Praise for *A Woman's Place*

"*A Woman's Place* will ignite a long overdue and healthy conversation in our churches about women and work. I loved this book, and I wish I could put it in the hands of every woman I know."

—Sarah Bessey, author of *Jesus Feminist*

"Whether you are a man or a woman, whether you work at school, an office, or home, *A Woman's Place* will inform, challenge, and inspire you."

—Karen Swallow Prior, Ph.D., author of *Booked: Literature in the Soul of Me*

"Insightful . . . Incisive commentary on how cultural mores have been overlaid on biblical texts should help the Christian community pry off those faulty, 'how-it-is' assumptions and free us to explore the reforms needed to get to 'how-it-ought-to-be.'"

—Amy L. Sherman, author of *Kingdom Calling*

"Women in all life stages will benefit from Katelyn Beaty's holistic and positive theology of work, whether that work is carpools or corporate board meetings—or both."

—Kara Powell, Ph.D., author of *Sticky Faith* and *Growing Young*

"As this excellent book evidences, a woman's place is throughout the culture. Indeed, where women are not present the world lacks its full depth."

—Dave Blanchard, cofounder and CEO of Praxis

"Whether you are a man or a woman, this will challenge your thinking and encourage you to a better and deeper view of vocation."

—Ed Stetzer, executive director of LifeWay Christian Resources of the Southern Baptist Convention

"Opens our eyes to the central place work has for every image bearer of God . . . A must-read book for both women and men."

—Tom Nelson, president of Made to Flourish

"With characteristic transparency, elegance, and prophetic strength, Katelyn Beaty has given us a book that I pray will have a profound influence on women and men alike."

—Scott Sauls, author of *Jesus Outside the Lines*

"Shows . . . what it means for women to take their places alongside men in fulfilling God's command to cultivate the world. . . . Convincingly calls each of us, female and male, to a wiser, fuller, and healthier life."

—John G. Stackhouse, Jr., Samuel J. Mikolaski
Professor of Religious Studies, Crandall University, Moncton, Canada

"Advocating for the empowerment of women to fulfill their God-given roles, Katelyn Beaty looks throughout Scripture and history for insights. What she finds is an encouragement to every woman who feels called to work—both inside and outside the home."

—D. Michael Lindsay, president of Gordon College

"Work is an essential part of being made in God's image, and women are essential image bearers. Katelyn Beaty's *A Woman's Place* brings reflection on Scripture and an informed mind to help answer the question implied in the title—a woman's place is to be an agent of shalom working with dignity and strength in all spheres of God's redemptive plan for a flourishing creation."

—John Ortberg, senior pastor of Menlo Park Presbyterian Church
and author of *All the Places to Go*, and Nancy Ortberg, CEO of
Transforming the Bay with Christ

"Long needed, Beaty offers a thoughtful integration of secular and Christian thought about the emerging possibilities and continued challenges facing women in America's professional workplace."

—Daniel W. Miller, director of Princeton University's Faith &
Work Initiative and president of the Avodah Institute

"A thoughtful biblical perspective on women and work has been long overdue, but thanks to Katelyn Beaty's excellent *A Woman's Place*, the wait is over. May this thorough and provocative treatment of a tremendously important subject find the widest possible audience."

—Eric Metaxas, *New York Times* bestselling author of *Bonhoeffer:
Pastor, Martyr, Prophet, Spy* and host of *The Eric Metaxas Show*

A WOMAN'S PLACE

A Christian Vision for Your Calling
in the Office, the Home, and the World

KATELYN BEATY

Foreword by Christine Caine

HOWARD BOOKS
An Imprint of Simon & Schuster, Inc.
New York   London   Toronto   Sydney   New Delhi

Howard Books
An Imprint of Simon & Schuster, Inc.
1230 Avenue of the Americas
New York, NY 10020

First Howard Books trade paper edition August 2017

HOWARD and colophon are trademarks of Simon & Schuster, Inc.

For information about special discounts for bulk purchases,
please contact Simon & Schuster Special Sales at 1-866-506-1949
or business@simonandschuster.com.

The Simon & Schuster Speakers Bureau can bring authors to your
live event. For more information or to book an event, contact
the Simon & Schuster Speakers Bureau at 1-866-248-3049
or visit our website at www.simonspeakers.com.

Manufactured in the United States of America

10   9   8   7   6   5   4   3   2

The Library of Congress has cataloged the hardcover edition as follows:

Names: Beaty, Katelyn, author.
Title: A woman's place: a Christian vision for your calling in the office, the
home, and the world / Katelyn Beaty.
Description: Nashville, TN: Howard Books, 2016. | Includes bibliographical
references and index.
Identifiers: LCCN 2015048793
Subjects: LCSH: Christian women—Religious life. | Christian women—
Employment.
Classification: LCC BV4527 .B393 2016 | DDC 261.8/8082—dc23 LC
record available at https://lccn.loc.gov/2015048793

ISBN 978-1-4767-9409-9
ISBN 978-1-4767-9415-0 (pbk)
ISBN 978-1-4767-9416-7 (ebook)

For Granny and Boompa, who said I was going places

CONTENTS

"Christine, why can't you be like the other girls? Why don't you play with dolls instead of spending so much time reading? That can't be healthy."

"Christine, stop playing soccer with the boys. You should be in the kitchen learning to cook."

"Why do you spend so much time on schoolwork? Boys don't like girls who are smarter than they are. No boy will want to marry you."

The message I heard as a young girl was loud and clear: A good Greek girl should want to learn to cook and play with dolls because her real purpose, her ultimate future, was to grow up, get married, and have babies.

When I turned seventeen, my family introduced me to a nice Greek man who owned a small grocery store. We fell in love, and he asked me to marry him. Then it was time to have the conversation with his parents. We Greeks like to keep everything in the family.

"Christine, if you go to university, you cannot marry our son," his mother said. "A woman cannot be more educated than her husband because she will not respect him. You must put away all of these foolish desires for further education and come and work full-time in the family business until you have babies, and then you can work part-time and I will look after the children for you."

So, it seemed that my mother had been right after all. If I wanted to fulfill the purpose for which I had been created, I would have to quench my passions and minimize who God created me to be. I could of course work as my own mother had worked for all of my life, as long as that work did not involve any kind of career or vocation that would take me away from getting married and having children. Work was a necessity to help the family budget, but it could not be a sacred calling or any part of my identity.

Needless to say, I did not end up marrying that man, and I spent many years trying to reconcile who God created me to be with the options I was offered. I could not understand why God would give us women gifts, talents, abilities, and desires if he had no intention of us using them for his glory in the world. Surely he did not derive joy from frustrating us?

I could not understand how we were supposed to reach the world with the gospel if we were not in the world and the workforce where we could share the gospel. Jesus said, "The harvest is plentiful but the workers are few. Ask the Lord of the harvest, therefore, to send out workers into his harvest field" (Matt. 9:37–38).

I could not understand how unpaid domestic work within the home was in any way more sacred than work outside the home. My understanding was that, "Whatever you do, work at it with all your heart, as working for the

Lord, not for human masters, since you know that you will receive an inheritance from the Lord as a reward. It is the Lord Christ you are serving" (Col. 3:23–24).

I could not understand how women could be the salt of the earth and the light of the world when we were confined exclusively to our homes and church buildings. Did Jesus not ask us to let our light shine before others, that they might see our good deeds and glorify our Father in heaven? (Matt. 5:16). Surely God would want as many people as possible, not just our immediate family and friends, to see our good deeds? This was about his glory.

At thirty years old, I ended up marrying a man who has relentlessly pushed me forward and encouraged me to be all that God called me to be and to do all God called me to do. Today I lead the A21 Campaign, a global anti-trafficking organization with offices in eleven nations, and Propel Women, an organization I founded to help women internalize a leadership identity and fulfill their passion, purpose, and potential.

I have come a long way from the girl trapped in a culture that severely limited my options as a woman, but it has not been an easy or smooth journey. The book you are holding in your hand is the book I wish I'd had when I was trying to understand why I did not "fit in" to my culture when I was growing up, or in the Christian subculture, when I became a follower of Jesus. I discovered that it was not only my possible mother-in-law who thought a woman should only want to marry and have kids, but that much of evangelical Christianity felt the same way.

In the fifty years I have been alive, there has been a

cataclysmic shift in attitudes toward women, work, and vo-cation. We now find women thrust into the marketplace but without a road map, trying to find their way through trial and error. Women are holding more leadership positions than ever before and yet they still wrestle with identifying themselves as leaders, owning their passion and purpose, or feeling empowered to operate with their full potential.

Katelyn has written a powerful and prophetic book that speaks to the angst that so many women feel. In it, she pro-vides a strong theological foundation that encourages us all to step into all that God has called us to do. She shows us the sacred value of work and that, biblically and histor-ically, women have always been involved in God's mission. She addresses the infamous Mommy Wars, the misunder-stood and often-overlooked single woman, and the married woman with children who believes there is still more for her. We can no longer ignore the fact that 57 percent of the U.S. workforce is female, and that 83 percent of women raising children work outside of the home. A great social upheaval in the twentieth century propelled women into the marketplace, and there is no going back. *A Woman's Place* elevates the conversation that must happen if we are to reach and engage a generation of young women with the gospel. Women have always worked, will always work, and are included in the work of God on this earth. Let's work together to make this work.

Christine Caine

A
WOMAN'S
PLACE

Let's Start at the Very Beginning

Like every great book in the world, this one starts with a reference to *The Sound of Music*. Specifically, with wisdom from the Mother Superior:

When God shuts a door, he opens a window—and launches you out of it like a cannonball.

This is more or less what happened to me at age twenty-seven. I had been an editor at *Christianity Today* magazine, based outside Chicago, for five years. I deeply enjoyed the work. I had cofounded a website that was reaching new audiences and starting new conversations for the church. And I was helping to lead a major three-year documentary series about Christians' work in urban centers. Doors of opportunity kept opening up.

I was also engaged to be married. Work was good for as long as it lasted. To be sure, growing up, I wasn't a girl who thought that life started on her wedding day. But I did assume that a Christian woman's life would proceed in an orderly, ordained fashion: Graduate from college, work for a while, get married, have babies, enjoy grandchildren, go to heaven.

Oh, sweet, naive twenty-seven-year-old Katelyn.

Needless to say, I did not get married in 2012. My life has not followed the script (one reinforced by Christian communities that mean well but will not find Scripture offering it as prescriptive). Watching my hope for marriage fall apart was nothing less than a trauma. But it also ignited some new thinking about work, calling, and living with purpose before God and others. As a Christian. As a woman. As a human being.

In the summer of 2012, on the same day that my engagement ended, I was offered the position of managing editor at *Christianity Today* magazine. Literally: On a Friday morning, over breakfast at the Red Apple Pancake House, without any forewarning, my supervisor asked if I would be interested in becoming the managing editor of the print magazine. Four hours later, my fiancé and I realized we could not get married and parted ways forever. In a matter of hours, I went from "this person's future wife" to "*Christianity Today's* youngest and first female print managing editor."

Okay, Lord. You have my attention.

* * *

My own life changed course in a time when the conversation about work is lively, in the church and in mainstream culture. Western Christians are talking about professional work with new energy and resources. Sermons, conferences, regional networks, and Bible studies are helping believers integrate their faith into their careers, and to honor Christ in all spheres of cultural enterprise. At its best, the "faith and work" conversation offers blessing and dignity to the surgeon and sanitation worker alike. This is all to the good, but the conversation hasn't fully reached the people who make up over half of every Christian tradition in America.

Meanwhile, women today inhabit every professional sphere, including ones long thought unbefitting their sex. In higher education and many fields of business, women now outnumber and outperform men. Yet for all their professional success, many women—especially Christian women—face unsettledness about their work. For them, professional work is something to justify, to others and to themselves. Something to couch in explanation or to downplay. Something that is good—up to a point.

This was confirmed in my research for this book. Over the course of a year, I hosted conversations with nine groups of women in eight different cities across the country (plus a conversation with students in England), eventually speaking with more than 120 women. I hosted the groups in order to ensure that this book reflected the needs and experiences of actual Christian women. To be sure, these women can't speak or stand in for all Christian women—they tended to be at least middle class, have a college degree, live in or just outside urban areas, and be white. But the sampling was significant enough to at least identify common themes.

Here is one common theme: First, almost to a person, the women I spoke with *liked* work. They all had gifts and aspirations for life beyond getting married, having children, and tending a home. A lot of them said baldly that they loved their jobs. As Katie Nienow, who directs a business start-up outside San Francisco, told me: "I can honestly say that I love finance . . . I love what I'm doing. In a lot of ways

I have flitted from thing I love to thing I love, and by nature of having been in places where I'm doing things that I'm good at, I have advanced in my career."

Another theme to emerge: For nearly all the women I spoke with, the desire to work came with a lot of *churning*. Very few of the women were fully at peace with work. Sometimes the churning came from within, from self-doubting questions—*Is this the* kind *of work I should be doing? Will working negatively affect my kids? Will work negatively affect my marriage prospects?* For many women, there was lingering guilt about professional aspirations. Here is how Tish Harrison Warren, an Anglican priest and writer in Austin, described it: "You don't want to feel like an ambitious wife is a burden, right?" Warren was quick to say that her husband very much supported her work. "It's more my internal sense of struggling with it."

And sometimes the churning was stirred up by others. Cecelia Cox is the vice president of marketing at Brit+Co, a creativity and lifestyle website in San Francisco. Six of the seven people on the executive team are women, and Cox says there's "lots of room for women's leadership." But earlier in life, in a time of anxiety over professional choices, a longtime male friend told her that she was anxious because she had a career, and "women weren't created to have careers." Even though Cox has received plenty of support since then, she says, "Unfortunately, it's that one line that plays over and over in my head."

Professional work has also been rolled into larger ideological skirmishes about parenting and what's best for children. The so-called Mommy Wars often pit "working mothers" against "stay-at-home mothers," even though most women I know find both labels inadequate to describe their daily lives. Even still, women's decisions about work come bundled in larger, exhausting debates about parenting choices that leave many women insecure and defensive.

Not a Plan B

I, too, have experienced churning around work. I have struggled to balance the demands of running a magazine with the demands of friendship, family, and church. (Yes, single people struggle with "balance"!) I have not always known how to supervise men. I have wondered whether women must choose between pursuing a career and pursuing marriage and family—and if I am foreclosing on one option. At least one well-meaning fellow Christian suggested as much (more on that in Chapter 7).

But at the end of the day, I rest in the belief that God really did open a window for me when a door was closing. That his invitation for me to work and to lead was not happenstance or a mistake, not good only as a plan B, but given as a direct and distinct blessing. Were it not for one dream ending, I might have missed out on another dream beginning.

This book is for all women who dream of taking their hands to the plow of life and creating something good. Something that will leave lasting goodness, truth, and beauty for this generation and generations to come. Something that will bless their neighbors and enrich their children's lives and satisfy their own souls. The desire and call to work is given to all people made in the image of God, who himself is a Worker and Creator (Gen. 1). And while all of us risk turning work into an idol, I believe most Christian women today run another risk: missing out on the goodness of work, on the ways that God intends to bless them and others through it.

"Every woman is a human being—one cannot repeat that too often," wrote the novelist and essayist Dorothy Sayers. (Ms. Dorothy is a bit of a spirit animal for me, so we'll hear more from her later.) "And a human must have occupation, if he or she is not to become a nuisance to the world." This is true whether you are married or single; whether or not you have children; whether you are well on a track of professional success or are just beginning to ask what you want to be when you grow up. If you are a woman human, this book is yours to hold, to pore over, and—I hope—to cherish.

K.B.

CHAPTER ONE

Made to Reign

Every human being is made to work. And since women are human beings, every woman is made to work.

On the surface, these two statements are fairly unremarkable. Scripture as well as human history tell us that all people in nearly all times and places have labored to provide for themselves, their families, and their communities. And most women in our Western context work for pay for many years if not for life.

But dig deeper, and these statements—especially the second—elicit follow-up questions. *Of course women are human beings, but what about gender differences? What kind of work does God give women to do? What if some women don't want to work? What about the value of unpaid work, especially motherhood?*

I wrote this book to answer these questions—to help women (as well as men!) explore God's invitation to women to labor for his honor, for their own enjoyment, and for others' benefit. I hope this book helps readers think about how to respond to that invitation. But before we explore *how* we work, we need to establish *why* we work.

For Christians, a good place to start is the Bible. In Chapter 3, we will look carefully at the Genesis account. Today, many sermons we hear about Genesis 1–3 focus on marriage and sexual intimacy, but in fact, the first pages of Scripture have a lot to say about work as well.

In this chapter, though, we start with a psalm (and not because that's where you land when you casually flip open your Bible).

Crowned with Glory And Honor

Psalm 8 is first and foremost about God: his majesty, glory, and power. But it is also about humankind: *their* majesty, glory, and power, a reflection of the God whose image they bear. In Verses 5 and 6, we read:

> *You made him a little lower than the heavenly beings,*
> *And crowned him with glory and honor.*
> *You made him ruler over the works of your hands;*
> *You put everything under his feet.*

These verses come to us from King David, who ruled for forty years over the people of Israel. But David is not describing just himself or just kings. And he's certainly not just describing men. When David says "him," he means "man" or "mankind." Which means that, in this passage of Scripture, David is describing all humans.

That means he is describing *you.*

In order to let this truth sink in, read these verses again.

But this time, replace the word "him"—which here means "mankind"—with your own name:

> *You made [Katelyn] a little lower than the heavenly*
>   *beings,*
> *And crowned [Katelyn] with glory and honor.*

The words inspire me to praise God for creating me to reflect his glory. God created the expanse of interstellar space, yet he hears me when I pray? There are currently 7.1 billion people on earth, yet he knows my own thoughts and desires better than I do? Like David, I marvel, *Who am I that you are mindful of* me?

> *You made [Katelyn] ruler over the works of your*
>   *hands;*
> *You put everything under [Katelyn's] feet.*

Verse 6 is even harder to grasp than Verse 5. And to be honest, it makes me squirm a bit. As a modern Westerner, far from the world of kings and queens, I'm uncomfortable with the idea that I am a "ruler." As a citizen of the United States—where everyone, in theory, is equal under the law—I'm uncomfortable with the thought of having power over other people. As a woman, I'm uncomfortable with power itself, because powerful women make us very nervous. And clearly not "everything" is under my feet.

But when I consider how I spend the majority of every week—as an editor overseeing the publication of a national Christian magazine—Psalm 8:6 starts to makes more sense. I *do* have rule, as weird as that sounds. With a red pen as my scepter, I survey countless words and thoughts. I protect what is beautiful and true and correct what is ugly and false. When a new issue comes out, I survey its boundaries, wondering if we should explore new terrain in the next issue. And in one sense, everything in the magazine *is* under my feet—meaning that when one of our readers is upset with our rule, the protest goes to me.

Psalm 8 helps us to remember a bedrock truth about *why* we work. We work in order to live into God's purposes for all of us: to reign over all of creation as his image bearers and representatives on earth. God intended all humans not just for relationships (with him, with others) but also for reigning—over every inch of creation. And whether you currently work full-time or part-time; whether you work out of a deep sense of calling or simply to make financial ends meet; whether you spend your days studying to earn a degree, or caring for small children, or managing a large staff; whether or not you even *want* to work, this truth is for you: You are called to "make something of the world."[1] To take your time, talent, resources, and community and create something good, something of lasting worth, usefulness, and beauty that will glorify God, make meaning out of chaos, and bless your neighbors.

So this is why we work, in the broadest sense of the

---

1. I am borrowing this phrase from Andy Crouch, who uses it throughout his 2008 book, *Culture Making,* and who is likewise borrowing it from cultural critic Ken Myers.

word. Before paychecks, promotions, and personal enjoyment, we work in order to properly bear the image of
God.

Our world comes to us because of the work of people
before us.

The World We Inherit

Take a moment to survey the room you are sitting in. Look at
the items in it—a chair, a computer, a smartphone, a stack
of books, a cup of coffee. Look even at the walls, the ceiling,
the windows drawing your gaze to the world outside. This is
the physical reality of your life. And if you traced the origins
of each item, you would find that every one exists because
of the labor and creativity of other people.

The items that fill our lives seem to appear ex nihilo
("out of nothing") at Target or at our front door, in a box
marked "Amazon." But every element of our material culture has an origin story. In our postindustrial global economy, they arrive through a series of decisions, emails and
spreadsheets, factory shifts, computer commands, and
shipping schedules (to name a few) that are executed by
people we will never know. And those people are building
off the tools and discoveries and labor of people who lived
before them. Our material culture spans not just across
oceans but also across time.

At the time of this writing, the newest iPhone—one of
the best or worst cultural artifacts of this century, depending on whom you ask—had debuted. I'll admit that when I
opened the box holding my new iPhone, I was blissfully

unaware of anything (or anyone) that had gone into making it. Like a child on Christmas morning, I was aware only of wanting to play with it right away. This is true for almost every physical artifact in my life and perhaps yours, too: I rarely think of the *why* behind the simple *what* of my life.

Yet everything there has been passed down in the warp and woof of human history. Nothing is a given, and nothing is random. That is true for material culture. That is true, too, for what we might call institutional culture: government and businesses and schools and churches and nonprofits and neighborhood associations—all gatherings of people who guide and govern the way we live together, from the most intimate gathering, the family, to the most impersonal, the state. What language I speak, where I live, how I get from one place to another, what movies and music I enjoy, what I believe about voting and baptism and green bean casserole—all speak to a world that I have inherited from other people and institutions.

Few others have contributed as much to Christians' understanding of culture as Andy Crouch, the author of *Culture Making: Recovering Our Creative Calling*. (For full disclosure, Andy is a colleague at *Christianity Today* magazine.) Culture, he notes,

> always and only comes from particular human acts
> of cultivation and creativity. We don't make Culture,
> we make omelets. We tell stories. We build hospi-
> tals. We pass laws. These specific products of cul-
> tivating and creating . . . are what eventually, over

time, become part of the framework of the world for future generations.[2]

So the world we inherit was sustained and created by the people before us, who had inherited the world before them. The only truly ex nihilo act in all of history belongs to God: the act of drawing forth the heavens and the earth and all that is in them from the "formless void." Everything that followed built upon the creative activity of someone else. To quote Crouch, "We live in the world that culture has made."[3]

The world that culture has made, the one that we all inherit, is built by men. So overwhelmingly so that we barely notice it.

"This Is a Man's World"

This is a man's world, this is a man's world
But it wouldn't be nothing, nothing without a
   woman or a girl

I wish I could somehow include in this book a recording of James Brown (or, let's face it, myself) singing "It's a Man's Man's Man's World," the Godfather of Soul's 1966 hit. It's unclear from the tone whether Brown was mourning the state of affairs or celebrating them.

But in fact, he didn't write the song. The lyrics were written by a woman inspired by the Bible.

---

2. Crouch, Andy. *Culture Making: Recovering Our Creative Calling* (Downers Grove, IL: InterVarsity Press), 28.

3. Ibid., 29.

Betty Jean Newsome was a former girlfriend of Brown's whom he had met at the famous Apollo Theater in Harlem. Newsome was inspired to write the lyrics after reading Genesis 2, in which God creates Eve out of Adam's rib. To Newsome, "It's a Man's Man's Man's World" is actually a gospel song, a meditation on the Lord's design. As she told *The Village Voice* in 2007:

> I was just reading the Bible and thinking about how wonderful and powerful man is . . . God, he can create, he can take man's rib out of his body and make a woman. I was just sitting there and thinking about how, after all of these things that he made and he did, all of it was worthless without a woman—and you gotta have them kids—or a girl. That's where the girl part comes in.[4]

Newsome's lyrics pack in a lot of truth. It is a bald fact that the majority of our material and institutional culture comes to us because of the work and creativity of men. Take the technology of the past 600 years: the printing press, the refrigerator, the lightbulb, the automobile, the phone, the computer—all the things that we can't imagine living without—were invented by men. The great philosophers and thinkers and teachers were men, by and large, as were the great political rulers; nations rose and fell because of the rule of men. The number of women who have contributed to these fields is, by comparison, so small that they

---

4. Clancy, Michael. "It's a Woman's World," *The Village Voice*, December 18, 2007.

are typically listed in women's history books. (See, when men do things, it's "history," but when women do things, it's special "feminine history.")

Of course, the situation has improved in the relatively recent past. Women today contribute enormously to the global economy. In most developing nations, women are key to sustaining financial growth and supporting families and communities. In the West, it is now accepted that women should be able to pursue education, and more leaders and politicians in developing countries are accepting this, too. Within the church, women are teaching the Bible, evangelizing the nations, and leading nonprofits.

And, to return to Newsome's lyrics, men would be "nothing without a woman or a girl." Even if women appear only rarely in the history books, none of us would exist without women. Men can make bridges and books and bombs, but they can't make babies.[5] And beyond their biological role, women in every time and place have "made something of the world," even if they were typically seen as bit players in men's stories rather than main players in their own.

But "This Is a Man's World" is true in another way: It accurately reflects a broken world, a world as it should *not* be. God never intended for men to reign over creation alone. He made all image bearers—men and women, who together reflect the image of God (Gen. 1:28)—to be his representatives on earth, to reign and rule over both material and institutional culture. It might be a man's world, but

---

5. Or, rather, their role in the work of physically bringing a child into the world is, by comparison, minute.

it was supposed to be a world governed by man and woman. And in societies like ours, where the locus of cultural influence is the marketplace (and no longer the home), women must be *in* the marketplace in order to shape material and institutional culture.

When the Psalm 8 call to exercise dominion falls more or less to only half the human population, then the creation—and fellow humans—fail to flourish.

The Male Lens

Since it affects all of our lives in one way or another, let's start with Hollywood. The film entertainment industry is the most powerful form of storytelling in our day, generating $564 *billion* since its mass-scale beginnings. About two of every three Americans will see a movie in the theater in a given year (not counting movies watched at home), compared with the one in two Americans who will read one book in a year. Movies have the power to ignite social movements, give balm to our souls (*Inside Out,* anyone?), and move us to great and noble deeds. When we go to the movies, what we are often watching is ourselves, reflected back to us.

And yet many of us *don't* see ourselves reflected back. The majority of today's movies—seven out of ten—center on the triumphs and trials of individual men. One study found that, of all the top-grossing movies of 2014, only 28 percent of all speaking characters were women. And it's no wonder why: Of all filmmakers—directors, writers, producers, cinematographers, and editors—an estimated 70 percent are men. When it comes to the role of director, the

rate is more like 95 percent. (There are also great disparities in the number of films created by directors from non-
white, non-L.A., and non-elite contexts: meaning the
number of films *about* people who aren't white, aren't from
either coast, and aren't highly educated are grossly lacking
as well.)

Here is how Laura Waters Hinson, an award-winning
documentary filmmaker based in Washington, D.C., described it to me:

> If you think about the fact that 95 percent of all
> movies you see are created through a male lens—
> that's a staggering thought. The vast majority of the
> media that we consume, that is shaping our souls
> in a lot of ways, is created by men. And I love men!
> But no wonder so much of it is violent or sexualized.

This gross imbalance matters not simply because "gender equity" matters as a modern ideal to check off a political correctness list. It matters because *stories matter*. Stories
literally change people's lives; it is no wonder that so much
of the Bible comes to us as a great story. We are story people. But when our stories reflect the experiences and views
of one segment of the population, we are missing a profound part of the human story. We begin to think of men as
the default human, even though Scripture teaches us otherwise.

Here is another example, one that has more harmful
effects than Hollywood films do. Today, the U.S. medical
system quietly minimizes or ignores women's particular biology and needs. Most of the people who participate in re-

search trials for heart disease and Alzheimer's are men. This means that diagnoses and treatments for these and other fatal diseases are shaped to respond to men's bodies—women's bodies less so. Women and men show different symptoms and need different treatments. But doctors are less capable of treating women when treatments presume a male body.[6]

Making matters worse, when women tell doctors they are experiencing pain, it is often explained as "emotions," "hormones," or some other "fake" or exaggerated display. For example, it usually takes people with an autoimmune disease on average five years and five different doctors to get the right diagnosis. And over 75 percent of those with autoimmune diseases are women. When a majority of doctors are men (68 percent in the U.S.), it makes sense they might not fully *see* the unique needs of women, despite all their training otherwise.

Beyond the West, we see a grave cost in countries where women do not reign alongside men. In 1994, when Rwanda descended into a genocide that lasted a hundred days and took about one million lives, very few women held political office. It wasn't until the early 1990s that Rwandan women could open a bank account, own land, or start a business without a husband's written consent. Girls were not sent to school and were considered valuable primarily as child brides.

It was only after the genocide—whose victims were

---

6. Dusenbery, Maya. "Is Medicine's Gender Bias Killing Young Women?" *Pacific Standard*, March 23, 2015.

overwhelmingly men—that women stepped up to the task of rebuilding the nation. Today, the East African nation is enjoying economic stability and peace, and women comprise 56 percent of its parliament. As one Rwandan leader said, "There's a general understanding and appreciation that if things are going to be better in Africa, women are going to have a key role."[7]

And this is true for every realm of culture, and every realm of work, in every part of the world. When our cultural artifacts and institutions are made or guided only or primarily by men, our world is stunted. Efficient, maybe. Containing beauty and truth and goodness, to be sure. But woefully incomplete.

At this point, let me say clearly: It's not that men *as men* are bad. Let me rephrase that: It's not that men are any worse than women! Men and women fall equally under the power of sin. The only thing sillier than believing that women are worse sinners than men is believing that women are better saints than men. Our world would have just as many problems if only women reigned, and it would likewise be woefully incomplete if only women reigned.

Let me also say here that power itself is not the problem. Again drawing from Crouch, we can understand *power* as the ability to steward, shape, and direct culture—from abstract institutions of business, religion, and law to the most tangible artifacts of food, buildings, and roads. To quote New York City pastor Tim Keller (who was para-

7. Olopade, Dayo. "The Fairer Leaders," *The New York Times*, July 10, 2012.

phrasing sociologist James Davison Hunter), "Culture is the power to define reality." Power is what God grants to all image bearers in Psalm 8. We all have some power.

But since the beginning of time, power and gender have been linked inextricably. And this is not how things were meant to be. In Genesis 1:27, we read:

> God created mankind in his own image,
> In the image of God he created them;
> Male and female he created them.

There is a reason God made us male and female. Maleness and femaleness are mysteries. And they can vary—sometimes widely—in how they are embodied and expressed, depending on place, time, and culture. But maleness and femaleness are good. Together, they bear the image of God; they bear the image of God, *together*. They are good not just because they allow people to make more people. Again, from Genesis, they are good because they help us to rule over creation, together:

> God blessed them and said to them, "Be fruitful and increase in number; fill the earth and subdue it. Rule over the fish in the sea and the birds in the sky and over every living creature that moves on the ground."

And this is ultimately *why* women are called to work, and why more women should work, and why more men should find ways to empower women—in Hollywood and the fields of medical research and business and the arts and politics and all other realms of human activity. Men can't rule over creation alone. "This is a man's world, but it would be nothing without a woman or girl."

The First Humanitarian Photographer

There are women throughout history who have responded to the call to rule and reign, even when the cards of culture were stacked against them.

The Bible itself is full of examples. Despite modern critiques that the Bible treats women as second-class, careful readers (or readers not laboring under a bad interpretation of Scripture) will note a number of women who exhibit strength, strategy, and stealth power, and who contributed positively to "the world culture has made" because of it. Queen Esther went undercover to save God's people from King Xerxes. Deborah was a prophetess and judge who consulted under a palm tree, where "the Israelites came to her to have their disputes decided" (Judges 4:5). Priscilla, alongside her husband, Aquila, was a tentmaker by trade whom Paul considered a "fellow worker in Christ Jesus." Lydia was a businesswoman who sold a unique purple dye—and made enough money to help bankroll the early apostles' missions. Yeah, it's quite possible we have a sugar mama in Scripture.

Plenty of other faithful women throughout history demonstrate, through their very lives, that families, industries, and entire nations benefit when women live into the Psalm 8 call to reign over creation. Oftentimes, their reign serves to undo the wreckage of a world ruled primarily by men. Such was the case for Alice Seeley Harris.

In 1870, the year Harris was born, Victorian England was enjoying unprecedented innovation, industry, and prosperity in every sector of society. Queen Victoria wielded authority on account of the royal throne, ruling over the largest empire the world had seen yet.

But though a woman wore the crown, British culture rested mostly on the power of men. Pervasive in the Victorian era was the notion of "separate spheres." Women, it was believed, were naturally suited to oversee the spheres of home and family life, and men were naturally suited to oversee the spheres of economic activity and civic life. Even the queen affirmed separate spheres—although she clearly defied them! As she wrote in a letter in 1870, "God created men and women different—then let them remain each in their own position."

But Harris apparently didn't feel restricted to the home when she married John Hobbis Harris in 1898. Before marrying, Alice worked at a London post office while training to be a missionary. It was one of the few professions of the time that allowed women to travel the world, sometimes alone. It was the great century of foreign Protestant missions, with William Carey in India, Hudson Taylor in mainland China, and David Livingstone in southern and central Africa leading the way. It was a time when Christian women were trained as teachers and doctors to use their skills on the mission field, so great the evangelistic need and so unprecedented the chance to travel.

The year they were married, the Harrises sailed to the Belgian Congo, a region in central Africa then controlled by King Leopold II of Belgium. Since 1885, Leopold had claimed the Congo Free State (CFS) as his personal property, ostensibly so that Christianity could take root in its basins and rain forests. Instead, Leopold turned the CFS into a labor camp and exploited its natural resources. An estimated ten million innocent Congolese died in Leopold's camps.

When Alice and John arrived in the Belgian Congo, they were shocked by the brutality of Belgian field officers—a brutality that would arrive at her mission's doorstep one day. Here is how author Judy Pollard Smith imagines the encounter, based on Alice's records:

> I could see that the young man at the front of the group was particularly devastated. His face was twisted in anguish. His friends led him forward by his elbows toward me. . . . The young man sank onto the porch and I thought he may collapse. He was carrying a small bundle bound about in plantain leaves. . . . I opened it with greater care than was usual because I was not sure what I was in for, given the way they looked at me with such burden etched on each face. To my own horror out fell two tiny pieces of human anatomy: a tiny child's foot, a tiny hand.[8]

The man, Nsala, had carried the remains of his five-year-old girl to the missionaries. His child had been killed by Belgian officers after Nsala failed to meet his quotas in the field.

---

8. Smith, Judy Pollard. *Don't Call Me Lady: The Journey of Lady Alice Seeley Harris* (Bloomington, IN: Abbott Press, 2014), 54.

In response, Alice did something remarkable, brave, even unwomanly for her time. She asked Nsala to pose, sitting on the veranda, looking down at the severed hand and foot of his child. Then she took a photograph using a portable Kodak camera, one of the first that could be loaded in daylight.

Even though Alice had no experience with photography, she began taking photos of other Congolese who had been mistreated. Then she sent the photos back to her host mission's agency as evidence of the violence in the field. Within five years, Alice's photos had circulated beyond the agency's magazine. The Harrises took the Harris Lantern Slide Show on tour throughout England and the United States, to garner support for their anti-slavery society. Ordinary citizens who had assumed that Leopold's rule was benevolent were given stark evidence of the carnage of colonialism.

One person who was profoundly affected by Alice's photos was Mark Twain. In 1905, he wrote a satirical pamphlet in the voice of King Leopold: "The Kodak has been a sole calamity for us. The most powerful enemy indeed . . . the only witness I couldn't bribe!" Some editions of *King Leopold's Soliloquy* include reprints of Alice's photo of Nsala.

The campaign against Leopold's rule in the CFS grew to a global hum. By 1908, control of the Congo had finally fallen to the Belgian government. Alice didn't work alone; she joined a vast network of journalists, activists, and other missionaries laboring to ensure that Leopold's violence was on display for the world to see. But the power of her photographs is hard to protest. As one UK journalist notes, "The fact that Leopold lost his unfettered control so soon after Alice's photos were made widely available to the public in Europe tells its own story." Today, Alice is remembered as the first photographer to campaign for human rights.

Oh, and she raised four children, too.

Making Work Work

We live in the world that culture has made. It's a culture that comes to us marked by Harris, whom we remember not only as a woman doing apparently unwomanly things but chiefly as a woman serving Christ, adding streams of his truth, love, and mercy to the flow of human history.

I first learned about her in a 2014 *Christianity Today* cover story—the most widely circulated cover story we have ever published.

In "The World the Missionaries Made," journalist Andrea Palpant Dilley presented the findings of sociologist Robert Woodberry. Over ten years, Woodberry ran a series of tests to measure the effect nineteenth-century missionaries like Harris had in developing nations. To his astonishment, he found that the missionary presence in the Congo, South Africa, China, and elsewhere was the *single greatest factor* in predicting the rise of democracy in those countries. That means economic growth, literacy, education (especially for women), low infant mortality, and health care—all marks of human flourishing. All marks of the whole creation flourishing when image bearers live into the Psalm 8 call to reign.

And you don't have to be a missionary in the traditional sense to live on mission in whatever professional field you inhabit. If the earth is the Lord's and everything in it—again to quote King David—there is truly no sphere of human activity that God isn't bent on reaching and remaking.

But for women to live on mission, we Christians need to massively rethink how we think and talk about work. In both subtle and not so subtle ways, Christian women are being discouraged from thinking of work as a good, direct way of bearing the image of God and living on mission for him.

First, despite new energy around the topic of work in some Christian circles, many still aren't talking about work, for men or women. Which is weird, since so many of us spend the majority of our waking hours at work. Julia Snyder, an educator in Philadelphia, told me that "everyone was a professional" at her former church in Boston, but, "there was no context in which people were talking about the effect that it was having on their faith." Because of this, she was more likely to talk to non-Christian peers about her work than Christian peers. This is a huge missed opportunity for the church to speak into a large part of most believers' lives.

Second, some Christian communities are talking about work in ways that are destructive and, frankly, unbiblical. One especially maddening example of this came from Liz Aleman. She serves on a legal team in Oakland, California, that advocates for children and teenagers in and out of court. At the office, she says, "I don't ever feel put down because I'm a woman." This has not always been the case. When she was twenty-two and excitedly told a pastor that she had been accepted into law school, "he said that I should consider the fact that no Christian man would want to marry a lawyer.

"This was heartbreaking, especially coming from a pastor whom everyone respected," says Aleman. "That is one of my deepest wounds, is the fear that Christian men won't like me because I'm a lawyer." In moments when some pastors and other spiritual leaders have a chance to bless women in their Psalm 8 call, they are cursing them, even as they think they are helping.

Other Christian communities simply don't know how to speak to the discipleship needs of high-powered women. This was true for Helen Young Hayes when she managed an $11 billion mutual fund in the 1990s. "The church did not know what to do with working women," she said. "There was a constant feeling of being less spiritual because I was full-time career, and much less spiritual when I was full-time heavy-duty career and I've got kids." Hayes experienced two stigmas at once: the stigma of working in the financial sector, and the stigma of working while having children.

Even at churches that don't teach that women shouldn't work while raising kids (and some churches do—we'll get to those teachings in Chapter 4), there are still subtle ways that working women remain outside the church fold. Jessica (who prefers anonymity) teaches college writing courses in Austin, Texas, and in 2007 founded a nonprofit that teaches Burmese refugees to make sellable handcrafted items. Jessica and her husband, Jonathan, have three children, and she says they are both "really committed to partnership," in their parenting as well as their ministry endeavors.

But every Sunday morning for five months, without fail, another woman at church would ask Jessica, "How do you manage it all?" As she told me in 2014, "I realized one day, no one ever asks my husband, 'How do you manage your time?'" It was assumed that Jessica was shouldering the parenting, home, and professional responsibilities all by herself, and probably struggling to do any of it well.

And some women really do shoulder most of these responsibilities. To a person, every woman I interviewed who is able to invest in professional work said she wouldn't be able to without her husband's full, active support. Not just verbal support but the kind of support that will cook dinner and do the laundry and take the kids to the grocery store. The kind that will bring a nursing baby to and from the office. Thankfully, many Christian men are laying down their lives for their wives in this way, fulfilling a husband's call to "love his wife as he loves himself" (Eph. 5:33).

Add into this already complex equation the endless debates over parenting styles; the lack of models and mentors; outdated workplace policies; a cultural fear of powerful women; and theology that teaches that secular work is less meaningful than ministry, and it seems nearly impossible for women to live into their Psalm 8 call on the job.

But it's not impossible—far from it. If the women I interviewed—as well as the eight women I profile in each of the following chapters—are any indication, more Christian women *are making work work,* for their families, their communities, and themselves. We could look askance at these women, wondering if they are neglecting their children or in the fatal grip of secular feminism. But I trust we'll let their stories speak for themselves—and, in the process, wonder what God is up to.

Laura Waters Hinson

*W*hen Laura Waters Hinson was a little girl, she would lock herself in her room and fall into a "creative flow."

"I would play the guitar for nine hours and take all my grandmother's evening gowns and hang them on the ceiling in formations," she says. "It was my space of creation, and I felt super-alive when I was creating." Somehow that got lost when Hinson went off to college, where she felt she needed to get a degree that would lead to a lucrative career. It took a breakup and what she calls a "come to Jesus moment" for Hinson to think through other options.

One of her mother's best friends from childhood was a Hollywood director who had worked on Madonna music videos and *Pet Sematary*. "She was the first person I had ever known doing this wild, creative work," she says. "I just had this sense of *Why don't I go to film school?*"

The creative risk has paid off. Today, with her company, Image Bearer Pictures, Hinson has directed and produced four documentary films. And though she didn't plan it this way, all of them have focused on the trials and triumphs of women. "Seeing a dearth of stories about women has compelled me to bring focus to these stories," she says.

Her first, *As We Forgive* (2008), follows two Rwan-

dans as they struggle to reconcile with the men who murdered their families in the 1994 genocide. Narrated by Mia Farrow, the film was shown to Congress and the World Bank, was featured in *National Geographic*'s film festival, and inspired new reconciliation efforts in Rwanda. The film showcases Hinson's desire to capture "how broken things could be made whole and put back together again and healed," she says.

While she steers away from the word "redemptive" due to its overuse in Christian filmmaking, that theme has shown up in her other films: *Dog Days* (2013), about an unemployed businessman who partners with an East African street vendor to launch a food cart in Washington, D.C.; *Many Beautiful Things* (2015), a profile of Lilias Trotter, who gives up a prestigious painting career in nineteenth-century England to become a missionary; and *Mama Rwanda*, a forthcoming film about "what happens when you empower a woman to start a business in an emerging economy," says Hinson.

Hinson has found a theme of redemption in her own story. When her first son, Riley, was born, she was committed to staying at home. "I just had this fantasy of myself as a stay-at-home mom; at the time, it was the only legitimate way to be a mother." That first year was hellish, she says; Riley was colicky and underweight and needed two surgeries for hernias. During that year, Hinson was alone all day—her husband pastors a church in Columbia Heights, a neighborhood in D.C.— and she thought, *I have died. My life is over.* "I couldn't

imagine how I could ever do creative work again and also be a good mom," she says.

Later that year, Hinson received a grant to start filming *Mama Rwanda* and relocated with her husband, her son, and her mother to the East African nation to film for a month. "That whole second year of Riley's life—not to be too dramatic—but it felt like a rebirth," she says. She and her husband had another boy, and while Laura didn't have any models for working while raising children, she figured out her own model. With support from her husband, out-of-town visits from her mother, and a nanny share, Hinson realized that her documentary work "doesn't have to die . . . in becoming who I think God made me to be, I'm going to be a better mother to my sons."

She says she has become a better filmmaker, too, as the demands of motherhood and creative work have forced her to use her time very efficiently. With some nudging from *Downton Abbey*'s Lady Mary—actress Michelle Dockery, who provided the voiceover for Trotter in *Many Beautiful Things*—Hinson is considering breaking into live-action film. "I'm not mad at Hollywood," she says, noting its wild dearth of women directors. "But I do want it to change."

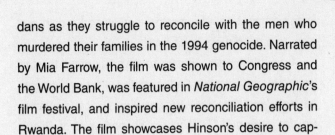

dans as they struggle to reconcile with the men who murdered their families in the 1994 genocide. Narrated by Mia Farrow, the film was shown to Congress and the World Bank, was featured in *National Geographic*'s film festival, and inspired new reconciliation efforts in Rwanda. The film showcases Hinson's desire to capture "how broken things could be made whole and put back together again and healed," she says.

While she steers away from the word "redemptive" due to its overuse in Christian filmmaking, that theme has shown up in her other films: *Dog Days* (2013), about an unemployed businessman who partners with an East African street vendor to launch a food cart in Washington, D.C.; *Many Beautiful Things* (2015), a profile of Lilias Trotter, who gives up a prestigious painting career in nineteenth-century England to become a missionary; and *Mama Rwanda,* a forthcoming film about "what happens when you empower a woman to start a business in an emerging economy," says Hinson.

Hinson has found a theme of redemption in her own story. When her first son, Riley, was born, she was committed to staying at home. "I just had this fantasy of myself as a stay-at-home mom; at the time, it was the only legitimate way to be a mother." That first year was hellish, she says; Riley was colicky and underweight and needed two surgeries for hernias. During that year, Hinson was alone all day—her husband pastors a church in Columbia Heights, a neighborhood in D.C.— and she thought, *I have died. My life is over.* "I couldn't

imagine how I could ever do creative work again and also be a good mom," she says.

Later that year, Hinson received a grant to start filming *Mama Rwanda* and relocated with her husband, her son, and her mother to the East African nation to film for a month. "That whole second year of Riley's life—not to be too dramatic—but it felt like a rebirth," she says. She and her husband had another boy, and while Laura didn't have any models for working while raising children, she figured out her own model. With support from her husband, out-of-town visits from her mother, and a nanny share, Hinson realized that her documentary work "doesn't have to die . . . in becoming who I think God made me to be, I'm going to be a better mother to my sons."

She says she has become a better filmmaker, too, as the demands of motherhood and creative work have forced her to use her time very efficiently. With some nudging from *Downton Abbey*'s Lady Mary—actress Michelle Dockery, who provided the voiceover for Trotter in *Many Beautiful Things*—Hinson is considering breaking into live-action film. "I'm not mad at Hollywood," she says, noting its wild dearth of women directors. "But I do want it to change."

CHAPTER TWO

Why "Leaning In" Is Good—And Not Enough

By some accounts, there has never been a better time than today to be a woman. Women of my generation have grown up in a time of rapid change in the Western workforce. And many of us grew up hearing powerful messages from mainstream culture about our capabilities and dreams. Before we explore the biblical story of work, we should explore the modern story of work. It's a story that has certainly shaped me, in one foundational way: When I was a child, there was never a time when I didn't imagine working one day.

I grew up in the 1990s, a decade when laminated posters on classroom walls told us to REACH FOR THE STARS and DREAM BIG against fluorescent night skies. "I can go anywhere! . . . I can be anything!" was the theme song of the classic PBS series *Reading Rainbow*. The song seemed to promise endless achievements, provided viewers believed in themselves and kept a positive attitude. I was born in the Reagan era, a time of "It's morning again, America" optimism and economic growth. And I came into the world during one of the most significant and enduring shifts in the U.S. workforce: Women were swooping into professions traditionally occupied by men. By 1990, the workforce was 47 percent female and 53 percent male, while about a hundred years prior, in 1900, it was 19 percent female and 81 percent male. America had finally woken up to women's ability not only to raise kids but also to raise the GDP.

It wasn't just that more and more women were working. It was that many women were crushing it: excelling at professions long considered off-limits to women or downright unfeminine. In fourth grade, I more than once checked out a book series in my elementary school library on sports stars. I learned about Billie Jean King, Mary Lou Retton, and Jackie Joyner-Kersee, all of whom had defied long-standing beliefs about women's sports prowess. The year I was born, Sandra Day O'Connor wielded a gavel in the highest court in the land, and Margaret "Iron Lady" Thatcher served as prime minister of the United Kingdom. In a fifth-grade project, I studied Judith Resnik, a fellow Ohioan who had died tragically alongside her crew members in the 1986 *Challenger* explosion. I learned that she had died doing what she loved: engineering and piloting for NASA, becoming the second U.S. woman to orbit the earth. How wonderful to imagine Resnik on the *Discovery* mission, peering down at the world God fashioned to inspire praise from men and women like her.

From these and other women, including my mother, I learned that to work outside the home was normal, even celebrated. I didn't grow up in an evangelical subculture— my parents became Christians when I was a young teenager, which was when I also came to Christ. So as a little girl, I never heard that my highest calling would be to have children and keep a home. I just assumed I would work—and also have children and keep a home—like all the women around me seemed to.

Apparently, one kind of work I wanted to pursue was selling real estate.

Early Aptitudes

On family vacations spent in the humid summers of West Michigan, I would retreat to the cool air of my grandparents' basement to watch the real estate channel. A syrupy voice guided viewers through the properties for sale, ticking off features while photos of local homes and condos flashed across the screen. At the time, I was blessedly ignorant of the minutiae of home ownership; this was long before the reality-TV home-improvement boom. But I liked the order of it all: the lot number, the bed/bath ratio, the prices. On a yellow legal pad scooped from my grandparents' kitchen, I took notes on each listing, imagining myself presenting the stats to buyers. I wanted to provide ordered, detailed information to people who needed it. (Because I was a big dork; we haven't yet talked about my subscription to *Cat Fancy*.)

A similar impulse must have inspired me to spend one morning in sixth grade job-shadowing at the local library. While my classmates were checking dogs' heartbeats and riding with pilots in airplanes across the Miami Valley, I was putting novels and magazines and movies on shelves. "You are so good at this," cooed one of the librarians. "We should hire you!" Dressed up in a denim skirt and Mary Janes, I beamed as I surveyed the fruits of the morning's labors: books once scattered now in their proper place, available for all. It was my own early Genesis act, bringing order to chaos, with some help from Melvil Dewey.

My mother was the person who had first taught me about the Dewey Decimal System. Like most other middle-class women growing up in the 1970s, she had graduated from college, the first woman in her family to do so. As an undergraduate studying library science, she was required to create a card catalog file index. Two oak filing drawers, their brass hooks designed for the crook of a pointer finger, held three-by-five index cards on which Mom had typed out all manner of bibliophemera. At age eight, I discovered her old filing drawers in our basement. I went to task creating cards for my own books, Angelina Ballerina finding a place next to an ungodly pack of Berenstain Bears.

My mom would go on to model for me that you could raise kids *and* pursue work that you enjoyed. Not long after my dad returned from Japan, where he had been stationed on a military base, she returned to library work. First part-time at a university library, then full-time at a public library in Ohio when my brother and I were old enough to stay home alone after school.

My mom didn't return to work for the money. My dad's career as a Marine Corps officer, then as a project manager at a construction company, covered our family's expenses. Besides, most librarians (except those at research universities or the Library of Congress) don't enter the field for the pay. It was a sheer love of books, children, and education that compelled my mom to work at a library, one of the few remaining institutions founded solely for the education and edification of all.

Why We Can Thank the Feminists

Like me, most of the women I interviewed for this book grew up believing they would and could work. Whether or not they grew up in a Christian environment, they were encouraged to figure out what they really enjoyed and dream about doing it.

"I wanted to be a police officer," said Lisa Etter Carlson, who directs a "neighborhood living room" in an underserved pocket of Portland. "I definitely have a sense of justice and wanting things to be right. At the heart of who I am, I'm very much a peacemaker."

"I remember making a shirt that said MOLLY FOR PRESIDENT," said Molly Sheffield, who runs a communications consulting business in Seattle. When she wrote this off as a "fourth-grade-type dream," the group reminded her that she had chaired a local university's alumni board, and that spoke to her confidence and innate leadership.

"I wanted to be a visual artist," said Hannah Faith Notess, who manages a magazine for Seattle Pacific University. "I'm happy when I'm in the zone making something. Right now that's my job. I'm happy when I get the finished product in my hands. That's a really rewarding feeling."

Even in the "very conservative, smallish Texas city" where she grew up, Micha Boyett Hohorst, a writer and mother based in San Francisco, said she knew from an early age—after a brief Amy Grant emulation—that she wanted to be a missionary. "I would have wanted to be a pastor if that had been an option for me," she said. But in Southern Baptist circles, "women could grow up and be missionaries. . . . The missionary thing was there all the way through college."

From an early age, these women and I learned that work was good and worth pursuing. I'm grateful that we did. Many Christian communities are nervous about the feminist movement: that it is destroying the family unit, or erasing gender differences, or undermining God's design for men and women. I understand some of the concerns. Even still, without the feminist movement—and women's broader entry into professional and public life—many Christian women would never be asked, "What do you want to be when you grow up?" We can be grateful for the *choices* given by feminism, even if we don't agree with every choice that every woman makes because of it.

However, we also take for granted the way every professional woman benefits on some level from previous battles for women to be treated fairly on the job. We forget it was only 200 years ago that women weren't allowed to pursue higher education, as the training of the mind was thought "unnatural" for women. Until 1962, it was perfectly legal to pay a woman less than a man for the same job because she was a woman. Women who were harassed or abused on the job had no legal recourse until 1964, under the federal Civil Rights Act. And as recently as 1972, employers had every legal right to lay off a woman once she became pregnant. Obviously, many workplaces today pay women unfairly, tolerate subtle forms of harassment, or inflict a motherhood penalty. But at least today we understand these things as problems that harm and dishonor women rather than "just the way things are."

If you have attended college; if you have worked outside the home for pay; if you have invested any time discerning your specific gifts and what type of work would best use your gifts; if you have advocated for a pay raise; if you have been given flextime after the birth of a child; if you simply have had a choice to both raise a family and stay invested in your line of work—then you can thank our female forebears. If professional work is an inherent good, then the women's rights movement has helped many of us realize it.

The Rise of the Alpha Wife

Today, for the first time in U.S. history, women hold over half of the nation's jobs. And these are not just bottom-rung or "helping" positions: Women hold 51 percent of all managerial/professional jobs, up from 26 percent in 1980. Over 60 percent of accountants are women, as are 45 percent of law firm associates. Though the top corporate jobs remain the bastion of men, with women composing just 3 to 6 percent of Fortune 500 CEOs, those women outearn their male counterparts by 43 percent. For every two American men who earn bachelor's degrees in a given year, three women will do the same. Even in places like India and China—

cultures with stronger traditional gender roles than modern America—women are running ahead of men. Women in developing parts of India are learning English more quickly than men in order to work in urban call centers; and more than 40 percent of private businesses in China are owned by women.[9]

Women are putting in more hours off the job as well. Today, the average American wife contributes 42.2 percent of her family's income, up from 2 to 6 percent in 1970. But she's not necessarily passing the diapers to her husband. In 1965, married women reported an average of 9.3 hours of paid work each week and about 10 hours of child care. By comparison, married women today do on average 23.2 hours of paid work each week, as well as *more* child care: 13.9 hours. Sociologist Arlie Hochschild has memorably called this phenomenon "the second shift," where working wives are still considered the primary parent as well as the keeper of domestic order.

Such demands on women's time and energy have given rise to so-called alpha wives such as Sarah Andrews, profiled by journalist Hanna Rosin in her 2012 book, *The End of Men: And the Rise of Women*. Sarah's husband, Steven, is a full-time stay-at-home dad, a phenomenon that would have been unintelligible to our grandfathers (and remains so in some Christian circles).[10] Steven sums up the new reality for many families: "I'm just the mediocre house dude."

---

9. Rosin, Hanna. *The End of Men: And the Rise of Women* (New York: Riverhead, 2012), 5.

10. Strachan, Owen. "Of 'Dad Moms' and 'Man Fails': An Essay on Men and Awesomeness," *The Journal for Biblical Manhood and Womanhood*, Spring 2012.

Sarah, a lawyer, "feed[s] the family" and "make[s] big money." She's the "superstar."[11]

Alpha wives and superstars are icons of women's swift advancement in the workplace and beyond. Women today encounter an enormous amount of "strong woman" messaging from the media. By many accounts, gender equality— the message if not the practice of it—is thoroughly mainstream. The maelstrom created by the 2014 firing of Jill Abramson, the first woman executive editor of *The New York Times*, demonstrated how much we now accept that women should be paid the same as men for the same job, and that gender should be no barrier to leadership, provided the skills and chutzpah are there for it. (Actually enacting gender parity, of course, is much harder.) Though it was disheartening to see one of the most influential journalists face apparent double standards and pay gaps, it was heartening to see people *talking* about it. We're attuned to the problems of workplace gender discrimination and have a vocabulary to address them.

Twitter campaigns of 2014, such as #YesAllWomen and #QuestionsForMen, ignited poignant online conversations about the misogyny that most women will experience at some point in their lives. TV shows like *Orange Is the New Black* and *Broad City* center on complex, funny, three-dimensional women (and, significantly, women of color) who can curse and beat people up and be just as sexual as typical male TV leads are. Even during a recent Super Bowl—a day typically centered on men's achievements and

---

11. Rosin. *The End of Men: And the Rise of Women*, 76.

the women who jump around them in short skirts—gender issues showed up, in the "Like a Girl" campaign as well as a PSA about domestic violence.

And then there is Beyoncé. Behold: Beyoncé.

Christians have and will continue to critique the feminist movement and its effects. But we would be unwise to simply wring our hands over feminism, then go back to our Christian bubbles. The reality is that feminism has defined broader cultural conversations about women's work and vocations because Christian communities have largely overlooked that conversation. If churches aren't grappling with the fact that women have professional ambitions and are already working, then we can hardly blame Christian women for turning to mainstream culture to honor those ambitions and speak into their daily lives.

The "Lean In" Moment

One of the most powerful voices leading the mainstream conversation belongs to Sheryl Sandberg. *Lean In: Women, Work, and the Will to Lead* is her incisive 2013 salvo that encourages women to plan, choose spouses, and work hard in order to secure top-level influence in the professional (primarily corporate) world. If we have inherited the world that men have made, *Lean In* is one call—sounded from the echelons of corporate business—for women to make something of that world.

As COO of Facebook, Sandberg is a Harvard MBA graduate with $1.3 billion in net worth. That means she is a world away from most women I know—most people I know. Yet her vision of a "truly equal world . . . where women ran half our countries and companies and men ran half our homes" is an attempt to address the problem that we reviewed in Chapter 1: that all image bearers are made to reign over both material and institutional culture, yet from the looks of things, primarily men do. Sandberg understands that "most leadership positions are held by men, so women don't expect to achieve them." She rightly underscores that "you can't be what you can't see," to quote educator Marian Wright Edelman. Meaning that we need more women in management and senior levels of leadership so that other, aspiring women know that they can do and be the same.

Sandberg notes many external barriers faced by working women, including negative perceptions of strong women. "The likeability factor" is a tightrope on which women who are direct and decisive are seen as difficult or aggressive, while women who are nice are seen as great administrators but not great leaders. Err on either side of how you self-present, and you fall off the thin tightrope to becoming a respected leader. It's no surprise that women's self-doubt and insecurity often sabotage any chance of moving forward.

Another reason the number of women leaders remains low in many workplaces, Sandberg notes, is because of bad policies for working mothers. The United States is the only industrialized nation in the world that doesn't have a federal paid maternity-leave policy.

Let me repeat this, because it's positively nutty: The richest and most powerful nation ever, in the whole world, ever, does not have a federal paid maternity-leave policy.

And because of such gaps in our workplaces' policies, many talented women "leave before they leave." "From an early age, girls get the message that they will have to choose between succeeding at work and being a good mother," writes Sandberg. Thus, many women tend to make many small decisions over time about children—sometimes long before they are close to having them—that slowly edge them out of workforce leadership.

On this front, biology doesn't help us; the time of life when many women need to board the baby train is also the time when they need to catch the career-leadership train. And because the baby train doesn't come back, while the career train sometimes does, many women choose to board the baby train. "The pipeline that supplies the educated workforce is chock-full of women at the entry level, but by the time that same pipeline is filling leadership positions, it is overwhelmingly stocked by men," Sandberg observes. She shares the startling statistic that, of Yale alumni who had reached age forty by the year 2000, 90 percent of the men were working, compared with just 56 percent of the women. "This exodus of highly educated women is a major contributor to the leadership gap," notes Sandberg.

Men, too, are unhappy about the setup. "Just as women feel that they bear the primary responsibility of caring for their children, many men feel that they bear the primary responsibility of supporting their families financially," writes Sandberg. "Their self-worth is tied mainly to their professional success." Notably, just as she reinvites women into corporate leadership, Sandberg reinvites men into hearth and home: "We need more men to sit at the table . . . the kitchen table." (Zing! More on this in Chapter 6.)

Notably—and contra those who assume she's denigrating family life—Sandberg praises the work of stay-at-home parents and acknowledges that many women "welcome the opportunity to get out of the rat race." She simply encourages women who love their work not to abandon it even while they love their children. Careful readers will find a clear pro-family message that urges more husbands and fathers to invest deeply in their homes and children even as they work outside the home. (More recently, in the book *Unfinished Business,* Anne-Marie Slaughter—the first woman public policy planner in the U.S. State Department—likewise affirmed parenting, or what she more broadly calls "caregiving." After lighting a match with her 2012 *Atlantic* essay, "Why Women Still Can't Have It All," she urges corporate America to adopt a more pro-family approach that accommodates mothers and fathers who want to prioritize parenting without being penalized.)

In fact, many Christian women are primed to affirm and build off the message of *Lean In*—especially if they have aspirations and gifts that don't fit comfortably within Christian subcultures. I can't count the number of times women have said to me that they gobbled up *Lean In* within a couple sittings or, like me, over a weekend.

"The night I began reading, I found myself feverishly earmarking and underlining," wrote Rebekah Lyons, cofounder of Q Ideas, a conference and Web forum for Christian leaders advancing the common good.[12] She wrote:

> Sandberg hooked me with her statement "We [women] hold ourselves back in ways both big and small, by lacking self confidence, by not raising our hands, and by pulling back when we should be leaning in." Agreed.
>
> As I sank deeper into our couch cushions, the moments followed with more outcries of "Yes!" as I resonated with her insights: "Women who participate in multiple roles actually have lower levels of anxiety and higher levels of mental well-being." Dead on. The past three years of my life confirmed the truth of that.

"Sure, I am the COO of exactly *nada*," wrote Lesa Engelthaler, senior associate at a Dallas recruiting firm for nonprofits. "And yet I felt a kinship with Sandberg from the first chapter as she described herself as a girl being called 'bossy' and knowing, even as a young child, that it was not a compliment." Katherine Leary Alsdorf founded the Center for Faith and Work at Redeemer Presbyterian Church in New York City and has led four tech companies throughout her career. She told me she sensed real truth in Sandberg's writing, especially in how she describes women's broken experience of work. "I thought [Sandberg] was very courageous," Alsdorf told me at the 2014 Gospel Coalition

12. Lyons, Rebekah. "Bravery vs. Ambition: Leaning Out, Not In," Qideas.org, April 5, 2013.

Women's Conference. "I thought, *Lord, I know you care about women. Sheryl may not know it, but I think you could be working through this book. It's time for this injustice and lack of stewardship of women's gifts to be resurfaced.*" Alsdorf noted that, like other landmark books that launched the 1960s women's movement, Sandberg rightly laments the ways many companies lose out when women aren't leading.

Lean In, as well as Betty Friedan's *The Feminine Mystique,* resonated with me deeply as a Christian and a woman. When Friedan describes "the problem that has no name"—the restlessness experienced by many middle-class housewives of the 1960s—I think of the pain and frustration that arises when our *Imago Dei* calls all of us, men and women, to tend and shape God's world, yet we find few creative outlets for doing so. When Friedan praises "the unique human capacity . . . to live not at the mercy of the world, but as a builder and designer of that world," I think I might be reading footnotes from the Book of Genesis translated into mid-twentieth-century parlance.

Likewise, when Sandberg writes no one—not even she herself—can "have it all" or "do it all," I think of the reality and goodness of our mortality and its limitations. That we have bodies and minds made to depend on their Creator rather than on sheer individual effort or day planners. And when she mourns the ways all of us have put women in stereotyped categories and expect them to think and act accordingly, I am grateful that God delights in giving his people a diversity of gifts (Rom. 12:5–8) and calls us to "outdo one another in showing honor" (Rom. 12:10), seeing and naming each other's unique contributions.

But there's at least one glaring omission in *Lean In*. And it's one that Christians are uniquely called to fill—if we have a right understanding of work.

The Why Behind the Work

When people learn I'm writing this book, one common response has been "Oh, kind of like *Lean In* by what's-her-name, Sharon Sanders?" (Okay, only one person said this.) The comparison is humbling as well as understandable, given the subject matter. But in the process of writing this book, I have bristled at the comparison. Why? Because Sandberg names the *how* of work—how to advocate for yourself and confidently lead meetings and navigate a company's flextime and maternity-leave policies—but only takes us to the far edge of the *why* of work. At the center of her sound and sage advice, and of the broader superstar messaging directed at women today, is a big gaping hole where the *purpose* of work, and of gender equality more broadly, should be.

I was abruptly awakened to the weakness of *Lean In* while leading a small group conversation at a Presbyterian church in southwest Seattle. To a group of about ten women, each with a distinct line of work and life trajectory, I explained the book project by mentioning *Lean In* as evidence that the topic of women's work was alive and well. One of the women in the room scoffed. "This whole conversation about getting the corner office—I have no interest in that," she said. "The women I work with are not thinking about any of this vocation stuff."

Over the course of the evening, the woman told us that she counseled immigrants from Mexico and Central America, many of whom had suffered sexual abuse and partner violence before coming to the United States. Now she was advocating for undocumented workers illegally detained in Tacoma, Washington. For her and the women she worked with and lived alongside, Sandberg's manifesto seemed focused on getting the already enormously well-off and elite members of society into even higher echelons of personal fulfillment. She rightly pointed out the way that *privilege*— the status and power conferred by society on someone because of race, class, education—intersects with our approach to work, convincing us that our own advancement is always the highest goal.

In reality, that's how most of mainstream culture—not just high-level corporate culture—thinks and talks about work.

Sandberg seems to imply that if any of us follows her advice, we can enjoy as much success as she has. But that assumes a whole lot about her audience members and their own place in life. She never acknowledges that to advocate for a pay raise or to speak up in meetings is privileged, for it assumes the protections of white-collar culture. It goes without saying that the choice to hire a nanny or a chef is available to very few people. (I've looked into it, but it's a bit outside my lifestyle choices right now.) The option of marrying a supportive man—a high-achieving powerhouse in his own right, yet one who is willing to split child care duties in half—is available to few people. Even to write a book (cough) is a choice that arises from privilege. It assumes an enormous amount of free time, support, and resources that people who are trying to make ends meet simply don't have.

Outside questions of privilege, most of us have inherited a flawed view of why women or men work at all. According to the mainstream secular narrative in the West, work is fundamentally about what it can give *you* rather than what you can give it. What it seemingly can give you is security, in the form of ever growing paychecks and an ample retirement nest egg; or affirmation, in the form of outranking colleagues or growing your Twitter following or gleaning awards or invites to exclusive events; or power, in the form of shaping a corporate culture and having others know how important you are. To be sure, security, affirmation, and power are not inherently bad. But they become bad—that is, idols—when we try to wrest them from our work rather than resting in God's perfect provision of all three.

This is ultimately why Sandberg's *Lean In,* and Rosin's *The End of Men,* and even Slaughter's *Unfinished Business* scratch a real felt need among many Christian women, but they really only scratch the surface. In their dream to see workplaces where 50 percent of all leadership positions are held by women, these writers have taken the dominant ways that *men* have treated work and baptized them in pink. None of these thought leaders examine closely enough the underlying values of the modern workplace—in large part because they have enjoyed to some degree the wealth and status that come with mastering it. Instead of questioning the world that privileged men in the West have created—a world in which career advancement is the highest goal—we women are simply being helped to acclimate to it.

In response to this, some Christians will discourage women from pursuing *any* professional success. *You should be content with what you have,* they will say. *Find ministry opportunities elsewhere. What makes you think God wants you to have it all, anyway?*

The Christian response to the blind spots of *Lean In,* and to the broader conversation that it epitomizes, is not to discourage women from pursuing professional work. It's not to imbue the homestead and motherhood with a holy, saccharine aura that hardly reflects the mundane, tiring, and at times downright boring aspects of either. The response is not to push all Christians to write off the workplace and become full-time pastors or missionaries. It's not to discourage all Christians from joining the corporate world.

The Christian response is to recover the holy, human, world-altering, and self-giving purposes of work itself. And for that, we leave the modern story of work and turn to the biblical story of work.

Ruth López Turley

*O*ftentimes our professional pathway is a way of addressing a brokenness in our own lives; we want to give others what we ourselves lack. Such is the case for Ruth López Turley, who is leading a large research project to address educational inequality in Texas.

Like students across the country, Houston's students perform well when their schools are well funded. When they are not, many students drop out, or aren't prepared or informed about college, and repeat a generational cycle of poverty. Not surprisingly, the education gap falls along racial and socioeconomic lines. "There are so many people in this country who are willing to work hard, very bright and hardworking," said Turley, who is Latina. "But they don't have the right resources and information."

Turley knows this firsthand. She grew up one of twelve children with a single mother in Laredo, Texas, on the border with Mexico. Her mother had six kids of her own and six from Turley's father from a previous marriage. With an eighth-grade education, her mother worked several jobs to make ends meet. "In my family, if you finished high school, it was a huge accomplishment," Turley said. "I almost ended up not going to college."

However, a guidance counselor noticed Turley's academic aptitude, and told her about a summer school

program at Harvard University for high school students to earn college credit. Turley was accepted. Because financial aid wasn't offered for summer school, she raised the money to go by writing letters and approaching local businessmen, and got help from her siblings. As a seventeen-year-old on Harvard's campus, she met Steve, and they both decided to apply to Stanford as undergraduates. Turley became a Christian at Stanford, getting baptized in a water fountain on campus, and she and Steve married at age nineteen, after their sophomore year.

Turley decided to study sociology because "I wanted to do something that could help address the problem that I had observed in my own childhood," she told me. Instead of becoming a teacher or guidance counselor, she wanted to understand why the education gap persists: "In order to fix these problems, you need to start by studying them, in order to know how best to chip away at them." Turley went on to earn her Ph.D. in sociology from Harvard University and received tenure at the University of Wisconsin–Madison. Still, even after landing a tenured position—the high-water mark for most academics—Turley felt deflated. "I could point to nothing that had changed as a result of my work."

In that season, now with two children, she began praying, *God, what is it that you want me to do?* Then she received a call from a private foundation in Houston. They wanted her to submit a grant proposal, asking her,

"What would you do if you had unlimited resources?" It was a spiritual awakening, not just a career boon:

> I ended up going on a personal retreat at a monastery, I spent time thinking about that question, and it helped me realize that if we are connected to God, we have unlimited resources. If we really believe God is all-powerful and can do anything, we should start asking him, "What is it that you want me to do?"

The question gave Turley the freedom—to the tune of $2.2 million—to brainstorm how her research could bring justice to U.S. classrooms.

Since 2011, Turley has directed the Houston Education Research Consortium (HERC), a partnership between Rice University and the Houston Independent School District (HISD). HISD is the largest public school system in Texas and the seventh largest in the United States. Turley's team of researchers evaluates the district's programs and studies macro-level processes such as identifying the strongest predictors of dropping out.

Turley's work addressing education inequality extends beyond the academy. When her pastor—Chris Seay at Ecclesia Church in Houston—learned about her work, he invited her to speak at the nondenominational church's five services over one weekend. Since

then, "Chris has given me several other opportunities to speak at church-sponsored conferences," says Turley. "I'm also an overseer at my church. I'm like the resident sociologist who helps the pastoral staff to think about sociological factors." In this way, Turley's work is supported by her church, but her church also benefits from her work.

Turley is quick to say that none of this would be possible without her "unusual husband." With a Ph.D. in church history, Steve Turley has had many full-time career offers, but he has chosen to work part-time (with InterVarsity Christian Fellowship) "so that he can focus on our kids and allow me to have a career." Turley continues:

> He has made the explicit decision that this is what works best in our family. There is no way that I would have the career that I have and children. You can't have it all, it doesn't come for free, it comes at a cost. He spends a lot of time taking care of the kids but also taking care of the household.

Turley believes more women academics could lead and direct efforts like HERC if "the church could do a far better job teaching and training men [how] to be a more active parent." Meanwhile, her own work is giving young women and men the chance to learn the value of an education and—like her—do far more than they thought possible.

CHAPTER THREE

Our Generous Worker God

The Bible gives us hundreds of names for God. And we hear many of them in church: Father, Counselor, Lord, Comforter, High Priest, King, Light. God has set up the world so that we can perceive him everywhere in our material reality. When we are loved and cared for by a good dad, we glimpse the love and care of our eternal Dad. When we are hungry and then satisfied by good food, we foretaste being eternally satisfied by the Bread of Life. Stand under a sturdy roof during a thunderstorm, and we sense that God is a Refuge. Watch a clematis climb a lattice and cover it with purple blooms, and we glimpse an abundant life on the Vine.

Despite all the names for God at our disposal, there is one I have never heard mentioned in church. And it's a weird one to miss, because it's one of the first images of God that the Bible gives us. The story of Scripture starts not with the story of God as Priest or Prophet or Pastor but with the story of God as Worker: "In the beginning God created." Our infinitely creative God wrests from the formless void land and sky and plants and trees and creatures of the air and creatures of the sea and livestock and wild animals and humans, all in a six-day workweek.

The crowning achievement of God's work is humanity, the only part of the emerging cosmos who bear his image:

> So God created mankind in his own image,
> In the image of God he created them;
> Male and female he created them. (Gen. 1:27)

In this verse, the Hebrew word for "mankind" is *adam*. It's a play on *adamah,* which means "ground" or "earth," so *adam* means something like "earth creature." Biblical scholars agree that, before the sexual differentiation described in Genesis 2, *adam* means "human beings." So we learn off the bat that God created human beings in his image, and that he created them as embodied, sexually distinct creatures. Together, male and female fully and cooperatively bear the image of God, and fully and cooperatively are invited to work like their Creator does.

When we compare the Hebrew God with other gods worshipped in the Ancient Near East, we find that the God of Scripture is utterly unique from those gods. One of his most unique features is that he *likes* work. In the book *Every Good Endeavor,* Redeemer Presbyterian Church pastor Tim Keller and coauthor Katherine Leary Alsdorf note that in other ancient mythologies, gods make humans so that they don't have to work; in these accounts, humans are like slaves, laboring for the gods against their will. By contrast, the God of Genesis is not too lofty or holy to work. Nor does he need humans in order to provide for or feed him, for he lacks nothing. Rather, he creates humans to partner with him to tend and oversee the world he has made.

"The God of Scripture is the 'great Worker.' He is more than willing to 'get his hands dirty' with mundane things," wrote the late theologian Gordon Spykman. "But he also stands ready to delegate responsibility."[13] Thus, Adam and Eve are appointed to care for the world. And when we act as stewards, caretakers, and administrators over God's world, serving him and others, we will naturally find joy and delight.

Though we might be tempted to imagine Eden as a place of leisure, in fact, it is a place of industry, even before Adam and Eve's rebellion against God. God places Adam in the Garden "to work and take care of it." He makes Eve as a "helper" in this work. So when we find ourselves fantasizing about a never-ending vacation—or inheriting Kardashian-esque levels of wealth so that we'd never have to work again—we are missing out on one of God's fundamental blessings to us.

What type of work does God give to his first image bearers?

> *"Be fruitful and increase in number;*
> *fill the earth and subdue it.*
> *Rule over the fish in the sea and the birds in the sky*
> *and over every living creature that moves on the*
> *   ground" (Gen. 1:28).*

---

13. Spykman, Gordon. *Reformational Theology: A New Paradigm for Doing Dogmatics* (Grand Rapids, MI: Eerdmans, 1992), 256.

The first humans are tasked with *increasing in number,* with *filling the earth* and *subduing it,* and with *ruling* over all the other creatures. God has planted the seeds of creation. Now he is handing over the tasks of maintaining and cultivating creation to his image bearers.

The Cultural Mandate—and Womandate

What a marvelous thought: With creative power beyond our imagining, God could have maintained the cosmos himself. The very act of creating the world and people to inhabit it is an incredible act of hospitality. But to invite people to create the world as well—to create many worlds, each with its own language and customs and tools and stories—speaks of a God unthreatened by his creatures, by letting them steward and develop his world.

It's a bit like a mother who invites her child to help cook a meal. The mom does not *need* her child to help; she knows that her child will slow down the process, get underfoot, and make a mess on the countertop. And yet she wants her child to know the joy of taking things of the earth—leaf, seed, grain, animal—and creating something entirely new, something that offers the world a bit more community, beauty, and delight. Also, she wants to be with her child. The invitation is about creating something together.

Or it's like Laura Streib, one of the first women I met through This Is Our City, a three-year *Christianity Today* project about calling, cultural change, and cities. Streib had grown up playing the piano, flute, and oboe, so she knew the joy of music from an early age. In 2006, she was earning a master's degree in music performance and working as a barista at Starbucks. But she noticed that, during the annual budget cuts in Portland public schools, arts programs were usually the first to go. So in 2007, she began hosting after-school art and music classes for children in under-resourced elementary schools. Since then, her nonprofit, Vibe of Portland, has grown to host forty weekly classes in eleven partner schools, where over half of the students live below the poverty line. For Streib, the classes are about inviting children to "play and wonder and excitement," she says. "Art education gives children that sense of dreaming and imagination" that's often lost when families and school administrators cannot make ends meet. She invites children to take the basic building blocks of our material world—colors and shapes and sound—and create things of beauty and delight.

Streib and her nonprofit provide one glimpse of what's called the creation (or cultural) mandate. The roots of the word "culture" are agricultural. *Cultura* in Latin means "cultivating," from *colere*, to "tend, guard, and cultivate." What God is asking the first humans to do in Genesis 1 is to tend and cultivate the world whose seeds he has already planted. Genesis 1:28 provides the general directive for human beings, while Genesis 2 colors in the specifics: tending the Garden (Verse 15), naming the livestock, birds, and wild animals (Verse 19), and receiving each other as man and woman, as close as bone on bone, in a one-flesh union (Verses 22–24).

Speaking of one-flesh unions: God, of course, intended

for the first humans to create more humans. I don't have babies, but whenever I spend time with one, I am amazed anew that God has enabled people to *create more people*— to put it in a much cruder way than do the Catholic theologians. While the other women at baby showers gush over the cuteness of tiny TOMS shoes, I am in the corner waxing philosophical: "Isn't it amazing that you *created a person*?" The procreative union between man and woman is a core way that we humans image the three-person God.

Yet it's clear from the Genesis text, and the church's engagement with it over the years, that humans are tasked with creating more than babies. God intends for them to build civilizations. Procreation is bedrock to society—you can't *have* a civilization without people to inhabit and guide it. But the buildings, food, laws, courts, gardens, clothes, calendars, dances, languages, and the million other artifacts and ideas that comprise culture are what God anticipates as he invites his image bearers to take up the creative task.

More Than a Feminine Touch

We also learn from the Genesis text that we cannot fulfill the creation mandate without each other.

It was not good for Adam to tend the Garden alone. So God gave him Eve, a "suitable helper." This helper was not an administrative assistant or even second in command. The Hebrew word for "suitable helper" is *ezer*. When this word appears in the Old Testament, it almost always refers to God *himself* as a strong deliverer in time of need. Andrew

Schmutzer and Alice Mathews of the Theology of Work Project note, "Genesis 2:18 describes Eve not only as a 'helper' but also as a 'partner.' The English word most often used today for someone who is both a helper and a partner is 'coworker.'"[14] Even that translation is imperfect, perhaps suggesting a purely task-oriented relationship—or an annoyance on the other side of the cubicle. But the word "coworker" rightly underscores that Adam and Eve were meant not just to live and grow a family together but to also work together.

Today, instead of two people living on a patch of fertile land near the Tigris and Euphrates rivers, we have more than 7.1 billion people vying for their own slice of cultural occupancy. Whether we see it or not, we depend on one another to live out the cultural mandate as did that first "flesh of my flesh" pair. The black plum that I ate for breakfast today bore a sticker labeled CHILE. The shirt I am wearing has a tag marked MADE IN JORDAN, a country whose exports to the United States grew by 324 percent over the past decade. The car I drove to the spot where I am now writing was designed in Japan, manufactured in either Ohio or Alabama, and sold in the Chicago suburbs. I just researched the location of Honda manufacturing plants using Wikipedia. There, I used the research and fact-checking of a disembodied but nonetheless real community made possible by the Internet—an emblem of our interconnectedness if ever there was one.

---

14. Schmutzer, Andrew, and Alice Mathews. "Genesis 1–11 and Work," *Theology of Work Bible Commentary*, https://www.theologyofwork.org/old-testament/genesis-1-11-and-work/.

In a very literal sense, every one of us survives on the backs of people who grow and harvest produce and raise and slaughter livestock—whether on a farm or in a factory—connected by the dizzying global web of food supply and demand. We survive by the sweat of contractors and construction workers who build our homes, which keep us safe against the elements. We are clothed by workers who often labor in unsafe conditions and are paid a pittance. Unfortunately, it sometimes takes a tragedy, such as the 2013 collapse of a Bangladesh garment factory that took the lives of more than eleven hundred people, for us to remember who—in very real way—provides our daily bread.

Strangers—in fact, the entire apparatus of society—depend on *our* work as well. "Work . . . yields far more in return upon our efforts than our particular jobs put in," wrote the late theologian Lester DeKoster. Work, he said, is what distinguishes human beings from the rest of creation:

> Imagine that everyone quits working right now! What happens? Civilized life quickly melts away. Food vanishes from the shelves, gas pumps dry up, streets are no longer patrolled, and fires burn out. Communication and transportation services end, and utilities go dead. Those who survive are soon huddled around campfires, sleeping in tents, and clothed in rags. The difference between barbarism and culture is, simply, work.[15]

---

15. DeKoster, Lester. *Work: The Meaning of Your Life* (Grand Rapids, MI: Christian Library Press, 1982). Quoted in *Every Good Endeavor.*

So we need each other, and each other's labor, to live humanely in the world. And not for the reasons we might think.

I once had a conversation with a colleague about the number of women who have joined the staff at *Christianity Today* magazine since I arrived in 2007. We agreed that the culture of *CT*—both inside the magazine and in our hallways—had changed as a result of the staff being a bit more balanced in its male-female ratio. This coworker compared the improvements at *CT* to the time during his college days when the dormitories became coed. "As soon as there were women living in the dorms," he said, "I noticed that there were all of a sudden fresh flowers in the foyer. It was so nice to have that feminine touch!"

I don't doubt that the dorms on his college's campuses looked better—and smelled better—once they became coed. The flower principle could probably be extended to other women and their contributions. It is the case that, whether due to nature or nurture or some combination thereof, women are generally quicker than men to think about aesthetics and hospitality. But when I say that we need women's work in order for our communities and workplaces to flourish, I don't have this kind of contribution in mind. I don't mean that all would go on as it has since the beginning of time but would now have a nice feminine touch. Rather, I mean that male and female bear the image of God together; *together* they bear the image of God. So when our cultural institutions only or primarily reflect the thinking and experiences of one gender, we move further from God's intentions for his image bearers. And what women bring to the table is not simply a feminine touch but half of humanity's gifts, passions, and experiences.

Soul Work

If we take Genesis 1–3 at face value, we also know that when women can't or don't "work with willing hands" (to paraphrase Proverbs 31), their *Imago Dei* is dimmed, and so is their own well-being. As Keller and Alsdorf write:

> Work is as much a basic human need as food, beauty, rest, friendship, prayer, and sexuality; it is not simply medicine but food for our soul. Without meaningful work we sense significant inner loss and emptiness. People who are cut off from work because of physical or other reasons quickly discover how much they need work to thrive emotionally, physically, and spiritually.

Almost all of us have a family member or friend who's gone without paid work since the 2008 recession. At the time of this writing, some four million Americans faced long-term unemployment (defined by the federal government as at least seven months without work). Senate members were debating whether to extend emergency insurance to 1.4 million of them. President Obama described such provisions as keeping the unemployed from "falling off a cliff."

The cliff is not just financial. Depression, anxiety, and overwhelming boredom can accompany lack of work. Those of us with too much on our job plates might dream of days on end to read and cook and play music without the interruption of deadlines and conference calls. But we would quickly find new work to do; there is a reason God gave us only one day out of seven to rest. "We invest so much of the meaning of our lives in our jobs," says Gene Veith, provost at Patrick Henry College and author of *God at Work*. "That's our identity, that's what gives our life reason, that's why we get up in the morning. When that is taken away, we feel purposeless." Since the recession, churches such as Menlo Park Presbyterian (California) and Christ Church of Oak Brook (Illinois) have started jobless ministries to walk with the unemployed during what ranks as one of the most stressful life experiences one can face.[16]

Many Christian nonprofits that fight poverty have learned that work is crucial to serving people in developing countries. For decades, the traditional charity model has called on Westerners to send money overseas to meet others' basic needs. This model has to a degree worked, especially for the poorest of the poor. But according to many ministry leaders—most notably, Robert Lupton in *Toxic Charity* and Steve Corbett and Brian Fikkert in *When Helping Hurts*—this model tends to overlook the innate gifts and industriousness of the people they are trying to serve. Arguably, the charity model leaves people in resource-poor countries *more* powerless and erodes their dignity as image bearers created for work. In response, many

---

16. Cooper, Elissa. "Blessed Are the Jobless: How Ministries Aid the Unemployed," *Christianity Today*, January 13, 2012.

nonprofits have retooled their approach to help the people they serve identify and use the resources they have, in the community, to be productive and steward the fruits of their labor. Work, it seems, is a fundamental way to preserve the dignity of all people, regardless of how much is in their bank account.

Yet even a voluntary departure from work can wear on our souls in unexpected ways.

Restless at Home

Some women I spoke to admitted that they experienced loss, depression, and lack of purpose when they left the workforce in order to stay home with their young children. "Admitted" because this seems not to be something that many Christian women feel free to say. We are supposed to be content once we have children. But after having children, should we expect to be *wholly* content with parenting alone?

Cindy Chang Mahlberg, raised in Colorado, graduated *cum laude* from the University of Pennsylvania Law School before practicing law in Colorado and New York. While in New York City, she explored the spiritual dimensions of her work through the Gotham Fellowship, a one-year program through the Center for Faith & Work (an affiliate of Redeemer Presbyterian Church). But she says that she did the opposite of what Sheryl Sandberg advises, and "leaned back" from her career, even before she and her husband had children. "I was afraid to pursue international business, which was my passion, because of the likely long hours and frequent travel, and I feared the implications it might have on my someday future family," she says. Rather than pursuing business and entrepreneurship, she found herself in a profession she didn't really enjoy, working eighty to one hundred hours a week.

But within the first two years after giving birth in 2010 and staying at home with her baby, "I spiraled," Mahlberg told me. She writes, "I had idealized and idolized motherhood. . . . I struggled both with a yearning to return to a full-time career and a sense of failure in not taking to motherhood more naturally." In other words, Mahlberg sensed a draw to work outside the home, yet wasn't sure if that desire was acceptable. Since then, she has launched a Denver-based social venture that helps other women integrate the dual calls to work and family. She also started a business that bridges her entrepreneurial passions with serving lawyers and other service providers.

Andrea Palpant Dilley can also speak to the loss involved when women leave the workforce. For nearly a decade, Andrea was a production manager for a small documentary film company in Spokane, Washington. When she became pregnant with her first child, "I loved the work and was hell-bent on continuing it." But the logistics soon became overwhelming; she was the first employee to ever try the work/parenting dual arrangement, and the company had no policy for it. (Yeah . . . more on that in Chapter 6.) Meanwhile, a freelance writing gig came along, and she decided to work from home. But, Andrea told me, "I love to work, and I still struggle with that now that I'm completely freelance. I love professional activity, I love intellectual stimulation. I could not imagine completely bailing out."

   We Christians have ways to talk about the joys of motherhood, and we should continue to do so. And certainly some women find *returning* to work as difficult as some women find leaving it. But we also need language to talk about joys of the kind that Andrea loves and misses. And when women voluntarily leave one kind of joy (paid work) for another (parenting), we need to recognize the loss as real, not as inherently selfish or careerist. We need to learn how to come alongside women who find the departure from work painful and even dehumanizing, because it is a departure from one profound way that they bear the image of God. If work is good and dignifying for men; if it is good and dignifying for people in developing countries receiving microloans to start their own businesses; if it is good and dignifying for college graduates landing their first job—then work is good and dignifying for the stay-at-home mother with three kids. We would be remiss not to see that.

The World's Toughest Job?

At this point, I hear the reader who spends her days at home chasing babies saying: "And who says I'm not working?" Up to this point, we have yet to define what we mean by "work" in a modern context, and what kind of work is implied in the Genesis cultural mandate. And we need to do so in order for women to grasp the kind of work they are meant to do.

   Going back to the biblical narrative, one simple definition comes from Genesis 2:15: "The Lord God took the man and put him in the Garden of Eden to work it and take care of it."

Adam's job assignment is to take his natural environment, labor to make it fruitful ("to work it"), and guard and preserve it out of love ("take care of it"). Here, work is simply what happens when humans interact with the created world for their own sustenance and benefit. This definition of work is wonderfully expansive. Clearly, work is not just what we do to earn a paycheck; it's not just what we use our college degrees for. It's certainly not just what brings us accolades or affirmation. So when women—and men, for that matter—labor to tend their garden or clean poopy diapers, they are no less living into the Genesis 1:28 cultural mandate than when they are, say, overseeing a legal case or writing a documentary script.

In this sense, when Mahlberg and Dilley stepped back from their careers to be home with children, they didn't stop *working*. Follow a woman caring for small kids for a day, and you'll witness a level of time management, strategic communication, and physical exertion that rivals that of some executives.

An Internet video released on Mother's Day 2014 imagined a hiring firm interviewing twenty-four candidates for a job vaguely titled "director of operations." Requirements and responsibilities included mobility—"the ability to work standing up most of the time . . . for 135 hours to unlimited hours a week"; excellent negotiation and interpersonal skills; degrees in medicine, finance, and the culinary arts; ability to work in constant chaos; and no vacation, with work ramping up during the holidays. Says the straight-faced interviewer, "If you had a life, we'd ask you to sort of give that life up—pro bono, completely for free." (Can you guess what the job description is for?) The #worldstoughestjob video, which was an ad for American Greetings cards, went viral, with nearly twenty-five million views. I imagine it did because it honored motherhood, a kind of work that is ubiquitous, crucial, and often under-appreciated.

"Family is culture at its smallest—and its most power-ful," writes Andy Crouch in *Culture Making*. Parenting is no less than the work of cultivating *persons*—growing them in physical, spiritual, and intellectual maturity, orienting them to the world through language and customs, and shaping them, by grace, to be the kind of people who will grow up to love and serve the Lord. Ask the world's most powerful leaders, people like Jorge Mario Bergoglio (Pope Francis) and Ellen Johnson Sirleaf (president of Liberia) and Bill and Melinda Gates, and many of them will trace their moral fortitude and vision to their parents.

Indeed, whatever creative labors we take, whether paid or unpaid, in the home or in the office, we can't help being what Crouch has memorably called "culture makers." "Making something of the world is of the very essence of what we are meant to be and do," writes Crouch. Our world-making will happen on the smallest to the largest scales of society—from the baby's room to the boardroom, from the dinner table to the district council meeting, from the neighborhood block party to the newspaper column. Just as there are dimensions to our work that go with and without remuneration, there are also private and public dimensions to our creative calling. And some of the most crucial work we do in our lives happens behind closed doors, without pay or praise.

And yet to a person, every woman I met while writing this book felt drawn, compelled, even called to a kind of work beyond her immediate family, as precious and important as those people are. Even women who were at home full-time and did not plan to work outside the home in the near future wondered what would come after the kids left home. And the kids almost always, someday, leave home. And the question of identity—*Lord, what did you put me on this earth to do?*—is still there, waiting to be answered.

One such woman is Janee Sedmak, whom I met at a gathering in McLean, Virginia. In a living room full of lawyers and public school teachers and one central policy adviser for former Speaker of the House John Boehner, Sedmak told how she had grown up "in a real conservative religious family" where, she said, "I didn't really know how to dream bigger than just getting married and having kids . . . or being married to a youth pastor or somebody in the ministry." After graduating from college, she met her husband, and within a year of marriage, they had their first child. "And it was something I'd been dreaming, my one little dream," she said. "And yet I was like, *Well, who am I? Now I'm a mom.* And then, of course, I had four more."

Today, Sedmak's youngest children are in high school, and many people have asked her what she will do with her time once they leave. In addition to serving on the board of a local school and on her church's healing prayer ministry, she says, "I'm really like, *Lord, I want to hear from you. I really want to be thinking kingdom thinking.* I'm beginning to just dream big for myself."

In many ways, women have not been encouraged to dream big enough. We have been led to believe that our calling and sphere of influence are private, while men's calling and sphere of influence are public. Beyond having no roots in Scripture, this public/private division leaves women not fully tasting the purposes of work. We were made to work not just for our families but also for our neighbors. And both the Sheryl Sandberg story of work and the contemporary Christian story of work given to women miss this fact.

Scales of Shalom

In the spring of 2010, my friend Sarah and I decided to host a feast. We didn't mean ordering some pizzas and texting our friends to come over. No, ours would be a meal of biblical proportions. It would take weeks to plan and several days to prepare. It would draw forth tears from our guests as they thought back to one of the best nights of their lives. "I want more and more plates to keep coming out," said Sarah as we planned the dinner at her kitchen table. "Just when everyone thinks that we're done, I want more plates of food to come out."

Sarah sent out handwritten invitations to twelve friends—people who didn't know each other but whom we thought should. We created a spreadsheet listing multiple courses, ingredients, and who was responsible for what. The day of the meal, a Saturday, I arranged tables and chairs in my living room, set out bouquets of roses and candles, and started to chop vegetables for the many appetizers and main courses. As the hour of the feast approached, Sarah and I grew anxious that we couldn't get it all done. There were a couple tears shed—and not of the sentimental sort.

But then the hour came, and we found twelve friends sitting in my apartment, passing plates of stuffed zucchini and spanakopita and orange slices drizzled with honey and cinnamon. Our guests stayed for hours, fulfilling Sarah's wishes that they would be amazed by how much food there was—peppers stuffed with couscous, kefta and zucchini kebabs, *bisteeya* (a savory Moroccan pie filled with chicken and almond filo), baklava. We talked about relationships, the best and worst jobs we ever had, our faith. Everyone left filled with good things, only one of which was food.

Another feast of sorts takes place every day at a restaurant in Englewood, a low-income neighborhood in Denver. There, Cathy Matthews serves her clients nutritious, tasty food—whether or not they can pay for it. Café 180 started when Matthews and a girlfriend visited SAME (So All May Eat) Café in 2010. They were meeting to discuss how to create transitional housing for the residents of Englewood. But they were fascinated by SAME Café's "pay what you can" model: Every item on the menu is listed without a price, so customers can choose how much to pay for each item. If customers can't pay, then they work in the restaurant in exchange for a meal.

With cofounder Libby Whitmore, Matthews opened Café 180 in 2010, and her restaurant has gone a long way to foster relationships between Denver residents from disparate backgrounds. "We drop off food and clothes, but there remains a barrier between the person giving and the person receiving," Matthews told *Christianity Today* in 2013. "What if there was more engagement? What would that relationship look like? How would it benefit both giver and receiver?"[17] By opening a pay-what-you-can restaurant, she saw a chance to meet immediate needs while creating unlikely bonds between the haves and have-nots. For five years, she has made healthy and in-season meals available to all, along the way forging friendships between the wealthy and poor, secular and Christian, young and old who volunteer together.

In some ways, what Matthews is doing in Denver, and what Sarah and I were doing in the Chicago suburbs, arose from the same good impulse. We all wanted to make and serve beautiful, delicious food. We wanted to foster friendships among the people we were feeding. We wanted to give those people a sweet, memorable experience.

Whenever we make a meal, we live out the Genesis 1:28 creation mandate. And when we make a meal that is healthful and delicious and unites people, we spread a bit of *shalom*. It's a Hebrew word that means "peace"—not just the absence of conflict but the spread of *flourishing, wholeness,* and *delight*. Cornelius Plantinga, Jr., former president of Calvin Theological Seminary, describes it as "a rich state

17. Haanen, Jeff. "Pay-What-You-Can Restaurants Dish Up Dignity in Denver," This Is Our City, *Christianity Today*, January 15, 2013, http://www.christianity today.com/thisisourcity/7thcity/pay-as-you-can-restaurants-dish-up-dignity-in -denver.html?paging=off.

of affairs in which natural needs are satisfied and natural gifts fruitfully employed, all under the arch of God's love."[18] Shalom is the way the world is supposed to be.

But shalom happens on different levels and different scales. And it's clear that Matthews could spread it a lot farther, into many more people's lives, than Sarah and I ever could. Matthews's work can begin to address large, often invisible, but very real systems of inequality, in a way that two women hosting a meal for twelve can't. Our feast could only ever be a private affair.

After the feast, one of our friends suggested that we try to host a second one. He said we should have it outside on the street and invite homeless men and women who spend time in downtown Glen Ellyn to join us. Our friend's instinct underscores the very nature of shalom: When we experience a taste of it, we naturally want to share it. But lacking money, time, and perhaps most important of all, institutional investment, Sarah and I never took his suggestion. Our feast was meaningful and good, but it had little power to spread shalom beyond the confines of our friend group.

Matthews's Café 180, by contrast, affects not only how Denver's poor are fed but also how Denver's affluent see the poor and reach out to them. Café 180 is a scalable model that, when operating well, can create wealth and lead to the launch of other pay-what-you-can restaurants. It can provide a livable wage to its employees, some of whom

18. Plantinga, Cornelius. *Engaging God's World: A Christian Vision of Faith, Learning, and Living.* (Grand Rapids, MI: Eerdmans, 2002).

may be able to escape the cycle of poverty, eventually not needing food handouts at all.

Ultimately, Matthews gets us Christians a lot closer to the purpose of work than Sarah and I did. Shalom is the missing piece in Sheryl Sandberg's vision of work. It is also the missing piece in Christian concepts of work that confine women to hearth and home. We were never meant to work just for ourselves or just for our families. We were meant to work so that flourishing, wholeness, and delight would spread to the furthest reaches of creation.

People who are captivated by God's love—expressed most fully in the giving of Jesus Christ for the salvation of the world—are free to pursue this shalom in whatever culture-making enterprise they undertake. When we are captivated by that love, giving our lives to God as an outflow of our gratitude, we become "prime citizens in the kingdom of God," writes Plantinga. We become people who are on a mission to pursue shalom in whatever sphere we are called to invest in.

When Christians are on mission pursuing shalom at the highest levels of cultural activity, they are acting as the *tsaddiqim*—a Hebrew word meaning "the righteous." As Amy Sherman, senior fellow at the Sagamore Institute for Policy Research, writes in her excellent book *Kingdom Calling*, the *tsaddiqim* (pronounced sa-da-KEEM) appear two hundred times throughout the Old Testament. A *tsaddiq*, or righteous person, is oriented toward God, working for him instead of for self and daily depending on the Spirit. The *tsaddiq* seeks personal righteousness, dealing with others with honesty and generosity, instinctively showing compassion to the hurting. She models what Sherman calls "social righteousness," seeking fair treatment of workers and customers. She eschews lavish living and prioritizes justice in her organization and broader professional field. Together, the *tsaddiqim* are ultimately the body of Christ out in the world—"people of deep personal piety and intense passion for the kingdom of God," writes Sherman. They return us to the richer meaning of work that our broader *Lean In*–type discussions miss.

The good news is that none of us has to become a pastor, a missionary, or even a social justice Christian to live as *tsaddaq* in our sphere of influence. We don't have to earn a degree in social work or public policy or go to seminary or move to the inner city in order for our work to matter in the kingdom of God.

Leah, a friend of mine from college, is a librarian at a large public library in the Philadelphia area. She was drawn to librarianship after undergrad because the library functions as "a sort of church," she told me. "It is a place where people come to be in community, to learn, to be edified." And just as churches attract all sorts of people, libraries are often the gathering places for people across divisions of education, class, and race; Leah says she encounters

the unemployed, the entrepreneur, the veteran, the immigrant, the bookworm, the spiritually hungry, the intellectually curious, the bored, the lonely, the tired, the sick, the self improver, the rich and the poor, the young and the old. To be in the position to help all people—uniquely available to literally anyone who has any need—is more than a vocation, it's a blessing.

For Leah, the chance to serve is the crux of her Christian calling.

Another friend, Kate, said she "always planned to go into ministry or work with a Christian nonprofit," but instead has taken on a demanding vice president role in the world of planning medical conferences, working for one company for fifteen years; she believes that's exactly where God has led her. Her career has been "the primary arena for discipleship and transformation," she says, "the place where I've been more challenged to grow in character, in conflict resolution, in practical ethics, in patience, in hope, and in perseverance." Even though the work itself has Kate interacting primarily with orthopedic and neurological surgeons—not the first people who come to mind when we think of the needy—Kate believes "any work can take on a spiritual dimension and meaning as we surrender it to the Lord and seek to please him in the way we carry it out."

Pam, a friend from church, is the kind of *tsaddiq* who understands her work to be her ministry but almost certainly wouldn't be able to carry it out in an official church setting. As a psychologist and licensed massage therapist, Pam sees many clients who have experienced physical abuse and trauma. She calls her work with them "an expression of healing prayer—many times Jesus healed people by touching them." Oftentimes her clients are dealing with "embodiment" issues, such as a disdain for their bodies or a fear that their sexuality makes them "unclean." "The questions and concerns that are brought to me are not the ones being addressed from most pulpits," says Pam. Her massage table is the place where she most directly practices pastoral care.

For women, the call to live as the *tsaddiqim* means that work brings with it not a nagging guilt or need to be justified, as if work were inherently "worldly" or taken up only for financial reasons. It means, especially for women, that work is a core way we honor God, serve others, and remember that our allegiance to Christ and his kingdom trumps our other allegiances and roles.

But for more women to live as the *tsaddiqim,* we will need to dismantle the notion that women are created to oversee hearth and home, while men are created to oversee the rest of the world. As it turns out, that notion is relatively new—and not one that most women have lived out.

Susanne Metaxas

*T*here is a great need among women in New York City for a listening ear and practical help when facing an unexpected pregnancy. Because many women don't find that, they choose to have an abortion. In 2012, 37 percent of all viable pregnancies in New York City—nearly two in five, twice the national average—were terminated.

In the early 1990s, a women's Bible study group from Redeemer Presbyterian Church decided to offer their neighbors other options. In 1996, the women launched the Midtown Pregnancy Support Center (MPSC), located near Grand Central Station. Two years ago, MPSC was relocated to Bryant Park and renamed Avail. The center provides free pregnancy tests, licensed counseling, and general information about pregnancy, birth, and abortion. The Christian affiliation is subtle, and the approach is open-handed; staff understand their job ultimately isn't to tell women what to do but to let them know they have options.

When Avail was launched, Susanne Metaxas was working as a senior manager at a cosmetics company but stepped away soon after she and her husband—speaker and best-selling author Eric Metaxas—had a daughter. After volunteering at Avail and joining its board, she started working there in large part because "I could choose my hours, which helped me to have a

young child and still be able to care for her and have a flexible schedule." Metaxas has been president/CEO of Avail for nine years. In that time, Avail has grown in staff size, volunteers, and services offered.

Metaxas believes that Avail's work is empowering in that it offers women choices that she says are not always given at Planned Parenthood and similar facilities. Over the course of counseling, "you realize that most women don't want to have an abortion. Most of our clients are either planning on having an abortion or considering one. But most women are not happy about it; they feel like it's their only choice."

Many clients are college students or young professionals and believe they can't financially support a child. Others are pressured by a boyfriend or partner to end the pregnancy. Avail's goal is to help a woman see that she has choices—and give her the practical help to realize them. That includes a supplemental day care program and a nurse-led pregnancy and infant-care classes. The nonprofit also provides post-abortion counseling, parenting classes, as well as adoption arrangements.

Ultimately, Avail takes a client-centered approach. While they do not refer for abortions, staff recognize that some clients will choose to have one. "We don't want to manipulate them in any way," said Metaxas. "We want to say, 'We are here, we support you . . . if you don't want to have this abortion, we are here.'" Though Avail refers for free ultrasounds and sonograms with a partner

clinic—Avail is not a medical center but a care network—
it does not use images of aborted fetuses to make its
case. Metaxas says this pro-life tactic "is not useful at all,"
often only adding trauma and alienating the client.

In 2015, Avail had 1,055 first-time clients and 1,796
client-care sessions. One client wrote in an independent online review:

> I found Avail on Google. . . . I was amazed
> that this whole operation is free to the pub-
> lic. More women should know about this
> place. I felt so comfortable during my ses-
> sions and the woman who helped me was
> nonjudgmental, friendly, and easy to talk to.

Indeed, Metaxas said, although Avail provides
counseling for men, women can empathize with other
women facing crisis pregnancies in a unique way. "Understanding how deep that connection is physically and
spiritually, with a woman and her child . . . I think every
woman can imagine the challenge confronted with an
unexpected pregnancy."

And that's why women like Metaxas may be one
of the strongest forces in today's pro-life movement. As
Marjorie Dannenfelser, president of the Susan B. An-
thony List, which helps to elect pro-life women to political office, said, "When men speak, people can hear the
intellectual argument, but they want to hear if there is
female support for the position."

Metaxas's leadership has also shaped Avail's work-place culture. Because she benefited from flexible arrangements while her daughter was young, "I really care about my staff having a flexible schedule," said Metaxas. "I can help women have a flexible work schedule, still be able to pick up their children from school, and have a job." As such, Avail is not just pro-life for unborn babies but also pro-family for its ten staff members and their families.

"By God's grace, we'd like to come to the point where no one is surprised that we exist, where everyone knows that if they or someone they know is faced with an unplanned pregnancy, there is help and hope," said Metaxas while accepting the Great Defender of Life Award alongside Eric in 2014. With a new location and the hope of opening several locations in the next five years, Metaxas will undoubtedly share that grace.

CHAPTER FOUR

Women Have Always Worked

From an early age, each of us is given icons of work. The mother who leaves at dawn for a long commute. The uncle who retires as a beloved schoolteacher. The older sister who endures working fast-food summers in order to save for college.

Mary Jean Beaty was my "granny," my father's mother. And while she never worked a day outside the home, she nonetheless gave me an early, vivid image of work done with excellence and care.

Nearly every month from when I was eight to eighteen, my parents, brother, and I would drive one hour to Cincinnati, Ohio, to visit Granny and Boompa for the day. Even though it was a three-bedroom ranch home, some fifteen hundred square feet, to me it *felt* like a farm. In the backyard grew tomatoes on the vines and bushes draped with blackberries. There was a greenhouse where lizards and bees and butterflies were preserved by the beating sun. Perennial flowers of every color and variety encircled the lawn; on the east side of the house was a beloved, fawned-over rose garden.

Granny tended things indoors as carefully as she did things outdoors. For most every room of the house, she had made multicolored rugs out of wool. The rug in the living room must have been at least twenty-five feet long and had left no scrap behind. A homespun afghan in red and white wool hung from the master bedroom wall; other throws and quilts were strewn throughout the home.

The center of Granny's best labors was the kitchen, the place where she mastered her most memorable work. Pies of every variety—banana cream, rhubarb, chocolate silk, apple, peach, pumpkin, and my favorite, coconut cream— would complete the equally memorable dinners, usually prepared from magazine clippings or *The Allardt Cookbook*. The latter was compiled by women of Allardt Presbyterian Church in Allardt, Tennessee, near where Granny and Boompa grew up and married at ages seventeen and twenty, respectively.

Granny died in 2009, three months after Boompa passed away. She had whittled down to a childlike fragility due to the slow onslaught of dementia. Married for seventy years, she and Boompa spent their final two years of life in an assisted-living facility. The transition to assisted care was difficult because it meant not only the loss of independence and vitality but also the loss of a *homestead*—a place of rest and respite where aunts and uncles and cousins had gathered for meals and holidays, a place of shared life and belonging. They had lived there for over fifty years.

As a teenager, Granny had worked briefly as a teller in the main bank in Jamestown, Tennessee. As was customary for many wives of the Depression Era, she didn't work outside the home for long once she married Luther Louis Beaty. They went on to have three children, the youngest of whom is my father. But it wouldn't be true to say she never *worked*. Her life was not that of the bored housewife sipping cocktails on the back porch. Nor was it the life of the mother whose every action and decision centered on her children. With tangible grit and shrewdness that contributed to the Beaty home economy, she labored "with willing hands," as Proverbs 31 describes the woman of virtue. For her eulogy, my father read aloud the passage describing "The Woman Who Fears the Lord," because Granny had lived it out so well.

Cultural Norms or Biblical Duty?

As we reviewed in Chapter 3, work is not just what we get paid for. Work happens whenever we interact with the created world, laboring to make it fruitful and beneficial to ourselves and others (Gen. 2:15). Women feeding and caring for young children are working. Men who are caretakers—like my dad, who watched over his aging parents in their final years—are working. Cooking a feast for friends is work. So is filling a home with blankets and tables and other items both useful and beautiful. "When we talk about work, we should talk about cultural contribution, not just financial remuneration [pay]," says Tom Nelson, senior pastor of Christ Community Church in Leawood, Kansas, and author of *Work Matters*.

To judge by this definition of work, women in every time and place have done it. They have always gathered and harvested and fetched and cooked and swept and spun, often with babies on their backs. Women in every era have provided a crucial economic backbone for their families, communities, and countries. In Chapter 1, we reviewed how absent women still are from the highest levels of public and political influence and why that is a problem. But alongside that truth is another truth: Most *men* who have ascended to the highest levels of public and political influence benefited greatly from women's work. "Behind every great man is a great woman," goes the saying. Here is another one: Behind every working man is a working woman. The difference is just that one of them is getting paid.

Some Christian communities today teach that women and work do not mix. Some pastors and Bible teachers believe that work will distract women from their primary call to bear and raise children; that it will emasculate their husbands; that it will lead them to have unnatural power over men at the workplace. Even more essential, we hear that women who draw their identity from professional work are going against God's design. Mary Kassian, an author who teaches at the Southern Baptist Theological Seminary, summed up this teaching well in a 2013 radio interview with Focus on the Family:

> You may have a job where you earn more money than your husband, and it may be practical for you to go out and earn the money and for him to stay home. But there's something in terms of identity that you're going against when you do that. God cre-

ated men to draw their identity from work. . . . God created woman to draw identity from relationships and networking. . . . Women have a unique and specific responsibility for the home in a way that men do not have.

I take such statements as sincere attempts to articulate the created differences between men and women, and the created goodness of maleness and femaleness. After all, leaders like Kassian believe that nothing less than the gospel is at stake when men's and women's distinct roles are blurred or confused. And there *are* real differences between men and women, observable across times and cultures, that inform how families balance work outside the home and work inside of it. For starters, only women lactate.

However, attaching manhood to work and womanhood to the home is a perfect example of well-meaning Christians confusing deeply bound cultural norms for biblical duty. And when such norms are elevated to spiritual prescriptive, so enter unfounded guilt and unfounded judgment. They have kept many women from pursuing work outside the home. And they have kept women from seeing the value of work they do inside of it.

The Disciples Had a Lady Bankroller

In order to address this misapplication, we need to look at what the Bible really says about work—specifically, women's work—so that we can figure out how these leaders over-stepped from cultural norm to biblical duty.

The New Testament is a good place to start. In his first letter to Timothy, Paul instructs his protégé to ensure that "younger widows marry, bear children, *manage their households,* and give the adversary no occasion for slander" (1 Tim. 5:11–14, emphasis mine). The Greek verb *oikodespoteo* appears throughout the Gospels for "manage the household" or "rule the household." This is a position of authority and responsibility, not passivity. Yes, Paul indirectly instructs these younger widows to be at home, but home is a place of industry, not idleness.

Likewise, in his letter to Titus, Paul instructs his friend to ensure that older women in the Christian community "train the young women to love their husbands and children, to be self-controlled, pure, *working at home,* kind, and submissive to their own husbands, that the word of God may not be reviled" (Titus 2:3–5). Our modern ears perk up to the word "home" and interpret it as the opposite of work; after all, we speak of working moms and stay-at-home moms today. But Paul shows himself to be rather forward-thinking here, as in other passages regarding women. He is indirectly instructing women who are new believers to invest in the foundational economic unit of their first-century world. As Carolyn McCulley and Nora Shank note in their book, *The Measure of Success,* "For Paul to counsel women to manage their households and work at home was to say women's work is important in both the physical and the spiritual realms. He was not limiting the scope of work for women today."

The New Testament provides other examples of the crucial role women's work played in advancing the gospel. There's evidence in the Gospels that Jesus and his disciples enjoyed the financial backing of Joanna, wife of Herod's steward Chuza, Susanna, and "many others" (Luke 8:1–3). "These women were helping to support them out of their own means." Lydia was a successful businesswoman as a "seller of purple" from Thyatira, and she opened her home and her finances to Paul and other early leaders in the church of Philippi. Phoebe, too, was a woman of means who became "a benefactor of many" for Paul and ministers in the church of Cenchreae. And even women who were not wealthy enough to be benefactors nonetheless participated in economic life in first-century Palestine. As Lynn H. Cohick, New Testament professor at Wheaton College, notes:

> We should imagine Prisca working alongside Aquila and Paul in their tent-making or leather-working. Perhaps Peter's wife sold the fish he caught. We must not imagine women, especially poor women (who, with poor men, made up the vast majority of the ancient world), tucked away in their homes, secluded from economic activity. Inscriptions, epitaphs, and visual art all suggest the active presence of women in the economy of the ancient world.[19]

---

19. Cohick, Lynn H. *Women in the World of the Earliest Christians: Illuminating Ancient Ways of Life* (Grand Rapids, MI: Baker Academic), 241.

And since we already mentioned the Proverbs 31 woman, let's look more carefully at how she's described, in Verses 10–31:

> An excellent wife who can find?
> She is far more precious than jewels.
> The heart of her husband trusts in her,
> and he will have no lack of gain.
> [12] She does him good, and not harm,
> all the days of her life.
> [13] She seeks wool and flax,
> and works with willing hands.
> [14] She is like the ships of the merchant;
> she brings her food from afar.
> [15] She rises while it is yet night
> and provides food for her household
> and portions for her maidens.
> [16] She considers a field and buys it;
> with the fruit of her hands she plants a vineyard.
> [17] She dresses herself with strength
> and makes her arms strong.
> [18] She perceives that her merchandise is profitable.
> Her lamp does not go out at night.
> [19] She puts her hands to the distaff,
> and her hands hold the spindle.
> [20] She opens her hand to the poor
> and reaches out her hands to the needy.
> [21] She is not afraid of snow for her household,
> for all her household are clothed in scarlet.

²² She makes bed coverings for herself;
her clothing is fine linen and purple.
²³ Her husband is known in the gates
when he sits among the elders of the land.
²⁴ She makes linen garments and sells them;
she delivers sashes to the merchant.
²⁵ Strength and dignity are her clothing,
and she laughs at the time to come.
²⁶ She opens her mouth with wisdom,
and the teaching of kindness is on her tongue.
²⁷ She looks well to the ways of her household
and does not eat the bread of idleness.
²⁸ Her children rise up and call her blessed;
her husband also, and he praises her:
²⁹ "Many women have done excellently,
but you surpass them all."
³⁰ Charm is deceitful, and beauty is vain,
but a woman who fears the LORD is to be praised.
³¹ Give her of the fruit of her hands,
and let her works praise her in the gates.

Whatever we believe about leadership in the home, or who should provide for a family, we can all agree on this: The lady *gets stuff done*. The Proverbs 31 woman "works with eager hands" (Verse 13), "gets up while it is still night" (Verse 15), feeds her family and female servants (Verse 15), buys and develops a vineyard (Verse 16), makes and sells linens (Verse 24), and oversees everything in her household (Verse 27). Today, she would be a seamstress, land developer, vintner, trader, and housekeeper in one—and a God-fearing wife and mother to boot. We seem to have found the one woman who "had it all," right here in the Old Testament.

As McCulley and Shank note in *The Measure of Success,* the Proverbs 31 woman is an "effective manager" who plays the long game. "She trades profitably so that she has earnings, and then she multiplies those earnings by buying a field and planting a vineyard—a long-term investment." She is shrewd and calculating. But she is also attuned to the needs of the poor (Verse 20). And the "fruit of her hands" is beautiful, inspiring praise at the city gates. "Most Christian women have heard plenty of messages about beauty," write McCulley and Shank, "but how many have heard it in the context of productivity?"

And how many of us have heard the Proverbs 31 woman highlighted in sermons or Bible studies for her *work*—her clear industry and productivity? We are more likely to hear that she is a devoted mother (even though her children are mentioned once) or an excellent wife (even though her husband is hanging out at the gates). If the Proverbs 31 woman were living today—in a Dallas suburb, say—she might face the following feedback from fellow believers, if not in words, then in sideways glances:

- *"She rises while it is yet night"? I mean, the work she's doing is great, but I worry about the kids. I just don't know how she has time for them.*

- *"She provides food for her household"? Um, why isn't her husband doing that as the provider?*

- *"She makes linen garments and sells them; she delivers sashes to the merchant." Yeah, she's really getting into this Etsy shop. Maybe to fund her shopping habit?*

- *"Many women do noble things, but [she surpasses] them all"? But how does she balance it all?*

- *"Her husband . . . sits among the elders of the land." Probably because he feels so emasculated at home.*

Some Christians have tried very hard to separate women from economic provision (or "breadwinning"). They teach that men are, in their essence, economic providers and women are home-based supporters and nurturers. With this interpretation of Scripture, the Proverbs 31 woman is praised for being at home—even though there was no workplace for her to go to. Her workplace was her home and the surrounding community.

The most definitive "women aren't breadwinners" teaching comes from pastor John Piper and theologian Wayne Grudem. In the classic text *Recovering Biblical Manhood and Womanhood* (1991), they teach that a husband's particular role is to provide economically for his family, and a wife's particular role is to be a mother and homemaker. Piper and Grudem base this thinking in the description of Adam's and Eve's respective curses after the Fall. Since Adam is cursed to toil in order to secure food (Gen. 3:17), we can deduce that manhood is inextricably tied to physical provision. Since Eve is cursed to painful childbirth (Gen. 3:16), we can deduce that womanhood is inextricably tied to being a wife and mother.

Piper and Grudem are very clear that rule is for all husbands and wives at all times. They write, "It will be helpful for all our discussion to keep this perspective in view and realize it is the perspective God has given and not some 'Victorian' or 'traditional' view that has grown up out of some society or culture and been adopted unwittingly as the Biblical norm." More recently, Owen Strachan, executive director of the Council on Biblical Manhood and Womanhood, affirmed this interpretation of Genesis 3 after a 2013 study found that a record 40 percent of U.S. mothers are the primary breadwinners in their families. (Of note: Over half of these women are single mothers.) Strachan lamented this trend because "In the Bible, men are not called to be workers at home. Women are. And women and even widows are called to marry, as the Lord allows, and then bear children and make a home." (Strachan later clarified that he does believe single women can work outside the home.)

Piper, Grudem, Strachan, and other Christian leaders are concerned about the effects of feminism on the family and gender roles—that women working outside the home usurp husbands' provisions and harm children in the process, or that women's professional aspirations denigrate motherhood and caretaking. The Council for Biblical Manhood and Womanhood was founded in 1991 expressly to counter feminism's influence in the evangelical church. But maybe it's not the Feminist Revolution of the 1960s and '70s that has undermined the family unit. Maybe it's the Industrial Revolution.

When Work Was Life and Life Was Work

"Working mothers" might be a distinctly modern phrase—a label thrown around for women to dismiss other women, or for politicians to pit female voters against each other. But it's not a modern phenomenon. From time immemorial, all mothers have worked. It's the stay-at-home mom—the woman who devotes herself *only* to raising kids and overseeing the household—who's the modern phenomenon.

The choice for women *not* to participate in the economic sphere of life is relatively new. All except the most elite women of society—aristocrats and heiresses, say—have had no choice *but* to work by the sweat of their brows. For most of human history, work was life and life was work. And men and women labored interdependently in order to provide the daily bread for kin and community alike. Only in recent history have men and women spent their days apart, with work on one hand and home on the other hand. Put your hands together, and you get the full historical view.

"Making a living" is a fitting phrase to recall here, for it underscores that work is intimately tied to our very existence. At the most basic level, it is the physical effort needed for a person, her family, and a community to survive. Of course, in our time, to make a living usually means performing a task requiring specialized knowledge, for pay, in order to buy the things we need and want. But for most humans throughout history, the order of the day was toiling "by the sweat of your brow . . . until you return to the ground" (Gen. 3:19). Jesus says we are to pray for God the

Father to give us our daily bread. Yet for the earliest communities mentioned in Scripture, daily bread would require their own sweaty, backbreaking work as well: plowing, sowing, reaping, threshing, winnowing, grinding, sifting, kneading, and baking. And that's just for bread.

Most humans who have ever lived belonged to an agrarian society. Sowing and harvesting crops, hunting, and husbanding animals for food and labor sustained families and communities. The Old Testament provides vivid descriptions of agrarian life. Land and vegetation and crops and flowing water are central to God's promises to Israel. Likewise, agriculture was the economic backbone of Palestine when Jesus healed and preached the Good News. The good and rocky soil in the Parable of the Sower, the crops in the parable of the wheat and tares, and the supersize barns in the parable of the rich fool would make sense only to an audience whose livelihood depended on the land.

Some anthropologists (and Christians) have looked to agrarian cultures to stress that men and women ought to work differently, even today. Because men tend to be physically stronger than women across time and cultures, and because women alone can bear and feed young children, men hunt game and women forage for plants and insects, keeping relatively close to home with the children. But evolutionary biology doesn't have the last word; anthropologists report successful female hunters and well-adjusted male gatherers. Further, it's not like women in hunter-gatherer societies stayed *passively* at home; historian Stephanie Coontz notes that they likely walked on average twelve miles a day, carrying anywhere from fifteen to thirty-three pounds of food home to their families. Some of them did so with a toddler in a sling on their back. Besides, as Christians, we will need better, deeper resources to understand the differences between the sexes than the claims of evolutionary biology.

How Separate Are Those Spheres?

In the history of North America, women cleared fields, planted crops, gardened, built lodges and tepees, collected wild plants and firewood, hauled water for cooking and cleaning, made bowls and other household items, and cared for young children. In the two-thousand-plus known Indian tribes and nations, men generally hunted, waged war, and led religious ceremonies, while women clearly got stuff done. So heavy was the women's workload that one Dutch missionary complained in 1644 that women were "obliged to prepare the Land . . . and do every Thing; the Men do nothing except hunting, fishing, and going to War against their Enemies."

Likewise, women of early colonial America ran the economic hub of life alongside their husbands. Married couples "inhabited the same universe, working side by side in a common enterprise (though not necessarily in identical tasks)," notes scholar Nancy Pearcey. Women planned and manufactured goods that were used inside the house and sold outside of it. What is more, men were deeply involved in child care; "parenting was not, as today, almost exclusively the mother's domain," observes Pearcey. Sermons and

parenting manuals of the day addressed both parents, and
fathers taught their children skills so they could pitch in at
home. Some historians observe that men gladly took up
what we now consider "feminine" tasks. According to John
Gillis:

> Males . . . were as comfortable in the kitchen as
> women, for they had responsibility for provisioning
> and managing the house. Until the nineteenth cen-
> tury, cookbooks and domestic conduct books were
> directed primarily to them, and they were as de-
> voted to décor as they were to hospitality.[20]

Today, such men might be labeled "man-fails"—a memorable name given by certain Christian leaders to men who
stay at home and do housework while their wives serve as
breadwinners.

Of course, this brief historical account hasn't mentioned millions of other women whose names and stories
are lost to history. For African-American women, the center of economic life wasn't their own home—it was other
people's homes. Slave women in the South worked on
other people's land; free blacks in the North did domestic
work in other people's homes. After the Civil War, the vast
majority of black women throughout the country continued to work in others' homes or on others' land, as domes-
tics ("the help") or sharecroppers. This continued all the
way up through the 1960s, when about 90 percent of

---

20. Gillis, John R. *A World of Their Own Making: History of Myth and Ritual in
Family Life* (Cambridge, MA: Harvard University Press, 1997).

black women in Southern states worked as domestic servants.

Immigrants who arrived in the United States after the Civil War through the 1930s also bolstered economic growth in this country. Traveling from Southern and Eastern Europe, China and Japan, these workers filled mills and factories to make clothing, other textiles, and glass. It was accepted that women ought to be paid less than men, so factory owners were especially keen to hire women from other countries who had little power to ask for more money or to work fewer hours. Not coincidentally, women played key roles in the labor reform movements of the late nineteenth and early twentieth centuries; they knew firsthand what it meant to toil like Adam did, by the sweat of his brow.

The Industrial Revolution reshaped not only how we do work but also how we do gender. And it—more than any specific biblical text—is the inspiration for the teaching that men are to be economic providers and women are to stay at home with children.

Between 1780 and 1830, the United States made a seismic transition, from an agrarian economy to an industrial economy. Factories replaced farms. Goods once made by home-based craftsmen—such as garments and shoes and pottery—were now made quickly and cheaply by machines. Factories and mills lured workers, men and women, into city centers with the promise of a living wage. While most Americans still lived on farms in the year 1900, the population in city centers grew in the last two decades of the nineteenth century by fifteen million people, many of them immigrants. And for the first time in history, the center of human productivity was no longer the home. It was the factory or mill and, later, for the middle class, the office.

Women of the working classes joined the rush to the cities. This included married women whose husbands were ill or misused their money; single women who sent earned money back home; and wives who simply wanted to contribute a little extra to the family budget. From 1865 to 1890, the number of American women earning wages tripled; by 1870, one of every four non-farm workers was a woman. Some mothers, most of them immigrants, worked the night shift, arriving home in the morning just as their children were waking up. Despite having husbands who worked, many of these women—like many women today—didn't have the luxury of choosing whether to stay home with children or work outside the home. Survival dictated that they choose the latter.

The story was quite different for the middle and upper classes. There, a powerful ideology was shaping family life and gender roles. The idea of separate spheres is, at the most basic level, a new way of organizing human culture. In it, business and finance are public spheres of life, and home and family are private. Today, when people talk about "work-life" balance for men and women, they are reflecting the legacy of separate spheres. Work is something that happens away from the home, away even from life, while "life"—rest, fitness, family time, spiritual development—is what we work *for*, even though ideally, we Christians should find much life in our daily work.

Separate spheres also separated men and women, husbands and wives, to spend much of their days apart. Men made the vast majority of the decisions in the public realms—politics, law, and business—and women made the vast majority of the decisions in the private realms—the household and family. Especially since work could be brutal and unfair, the household became a refuge from the physical and moral darkness of the world "out there." Women became responsible for maintaining the spiritual purity of the home. And men, writes Pearcey, "gave up their previous position as parental and religious leaders in their families. They simply were not physically present in the home enough to tend to the daily, continuous work of training and disciplining their children."

Separate spheres were observed in the United States as early as 1835. That year, Alexis de Tocqueville published *Democracy in America,* a travelogue of life and its peculiarities in the budding nation. "In no country has such constant care been taken as in America to trace two clearly distinct lines of action for the two sexes and to make them keep pace one with the other, but in two pathways that are always different," wrote Tocqueville. He observed that when a young woman married, "the inexorable opinion of the public carefully circumscribes [her] within the narrow circle of domestic interests and duties." The idea that "a woman's place is in the home" can be found in ancient Greek culture, traditional Judaism, and Christianity. But it became enshrined as moral and spiritual fact among relatively wealthy Americans in the nineteenth century.

Meanwhile, a lot of the creative work of home—sewing, preserving, baking, brewing—was moved out of the home and into the factory. Women staying at home found that much of the work of running a household was taken care of elsewhere. So motherhood became a profession unto itself, expected to take up more and more time and energy. Fatherhood, by comparison, became less of a duty for men. Pearcey notes that in this era, for the first time, "we find sermons and pamphlets on the topic of child-rearing addressed to 'mothers' rather than to 'parents.'"

Men also became breadwinners, a relatively new word (circa 1818) for the person who works to support a family or community. Having a wife at home marked men's financial achievement and entry into the middle class. Unlike the lower classes, these men could support an entire family on a single wage. For a long time, the ultimate status symbol wasn't driving a Beemer. It was having a "housewife."

After the Revolution

Where do we go now? Obviously, there is no turning back the Industrial Revolution. We can be grateful for the enormous wealth it created, and the enormous time and energy it gave us. But we are also wise to name its costs—and to name the ways we have let it seep into our teaching and interpretation of Scripture.

One cost of the Industrial Revolution and separate spheres is an enormous pressure on men to provide for their families, with little outside help. It used to be that a man would oversee the entire operation at his home, working alongside his wife, children, and neighbors to make ends meet. Now many men spend the entire day away from their families. According to a 2012 study, 60 percent of U.S. fathers reported experiencing work-family conflict, which makes sense in our so-called work-more economy. We expect more from men both on the job and at home; remember how much the men of *Mad Men* drank?

Meanwhile, the cost on women of the Industrial Revolution and separate spheres is legion. Since we are on the topic of *Mad Men,* let us recall Betty Draper, wife of the series' anti-hero, Don Draper. Betty has achieved the dream of many women of her time and class. She married a financially successful man and has a lovely and large suburban home away from the dangers and darkness of the city. She has two children and enduring physical beauty at age thirty-four. She is also strangely, crushingly miserable. Betty fills her days with cooking and cleaning and the occasional conversation with neighbors. The Drapers' maid does much of the housework, and many days, Betty sits alone at the kitchen table, smoking and staring into space. As the series continues, we learn that Betty is unhappy in large part because her husband is having affairs. We could diagnose Betty's (and Don's) symptoms as those of people who are spiritually empty and longing to be fed. We also should sympathize with

Betty. No human, male or female, was meant to live a life full of leisure and free of industry.

Another effect of the Industrial Revolution on women is that too much has been made of motherhood. Now, before you toss this book across the room, let me clarify: We can't make too much of *children,* of their care and development. The work of raising kids is unglamorous, difficult, beautiful, and crucial. Most mothers (and fathers, for that matter) I know would say that raising young kids is one of the greatest gifts and most important investments of this life.

But you can charge motherhood with a holy glow that breeds deep inadequacy and leaves women alienated— from their husbands, themselves, and other women. In what sociologists call "the professionalization of motherhood," along with the Industrial Revolution came a bevy of child-rearing experts, each dispensing strategies for raising healthy and well-rounded children. Parenting became a full-time job, something that a woman could study and perfect with the aid of the latest scientific discoveries. Go down the parenting aisle of your local bookstore—or Google "mommy blog"—and you'll see that our desire for the best mothering strategies is alive and well.

The problem with this approach is that motherhood is not a science but an art. More accurately, it's a relationship. And the more we treat it like a science, the more we judge each other's parenting choices and fuel envy, comparison, and pride. It's obvious that work can become an idol, a source of ultimate meaning that replaces God. But motherhood can also become an idol—a source of identity and self-worth that will not last. It's just that we are unlikely to hear motherhood described this way, so highly is it esteemed in many Christian communities.

It is no coincidence that the first wave of feminism came on the heels of the Industrial Revolution. Women were seeing the negative effects of alcoholism, promiscuity, and inhumane labor conditions in their families and communities, yet their influence was confined to the sphere of home. Rightly, they wanted to right social wrongs and improve the quality of life for their neighbors.

Likewise, the second wave of feminism—the wave that most bothers Christians—crashed into Western culture in the 1960s, because stay-at-home mothers were whispering, "This is not enough." "Feminism could not have captured the attention it has were it not tapping into feelings widespread among American women," writes Pearcey.

But Christians who are worried about feminism's influence, or about the breakdown of the family, will not have much luck telling married women to stop working. Women are already working—in the home, outside of it, for their families, for their neighbors, for the glory of God. Often these women are working because they have no other choice. It's worth repeating: The charge for women not to work outside the home, or avoid it if not financially necessary, is a charge bound by *privilege*. Mothers of the poor and working classes can't choose to stay at home. And if economic dependence on a husband is a quintessential mark of womanhood, are single women or childless women or widowed women not quite women?

When a description of universal womanhood begins to

apply to a smaller and smaller slice of people, we have to ask whether that description can be truly universal. When we have to make a list of exceptions to apply a model of womanhood, it is good to ask whether that model holds much meaning. Here are some exceptions to the teaching that husbands are created to provide financially and wives are created to stay at home:

- women whose husbands cannot work due to disability or injury;

- women whose husbands squander or misuse the family finances if given charge over them (a common problem in many developing countries, by the way);

- women who, alongside their husbands, find it nearly impossible to raise a family on one budget;

- women whose call to missionary work or evangelism regularly takes them outside the home;

- women who cannot have children or whose children are grown and have left home;

- and the majority of women throughout history who have had to work, for to work has almost always meant to survive.

Calling work masculine and relationships and networking feminine, as Mary Kassian has, threatens to keep women from knowing the good and holy purposes of work, whether inside the home or outside of it. Ultimately, such teachings keep women from understanding a crucial part of bearing God's image. By managing her household with endless thrift and creativity, my granny bore the image of our creative, working God in a beautiful and lasting way. Whether we work outside the home or inside of it, we could all stand to learn from her.

*M*ost Christians in the affluent West have bought a bag of fair-trade coffee, a pair of shoes, or a necklace at a church bazaar to support people in other parts of the world. "Business as mission" (BAM) is an umbrella term for companies that aim to bring both spiritual and economic growth to developing countries. BAM businesses fit into a recent boom of companies that identify social good as one of their bottom lines.

Jessica Honegger, thirty-nine, is the founder and co-CEO of such a company. Noonday Collection, founded in 2010, sells accessories made by artisans in Latin America, East Africa, and Asia. As of today, Noonday employs more than two thousand jewelry makers, who use their earnings to send their children to school and reinvest in their communities.

Honegger is also providing fellow women in the United States a business as mission—that of tasting the satisfaction of entrepreneurship. And it's working: In 2014, Noonday earned $11 million in revenue and saw a three-year growth rate of over 5,000 percent. It recently appeared as number three on *Inc.*'s list of the fastest-growing companies run by women, and forty-five among fastest-growing companies overall.

Honegger displayed an entrepreneurial streak at a young age. While other girls were setting up lemonade stands, she was hosting jewelry stands. A San Antonio

native, she grew up surrounded by fashion mavens. "I come from a long line of jewelry wearers," Honegger told *Christianity Today* editor Kate Shellnutt in 2015. "My earliest memories of my grandma are of going jewelry shopping with her, and my mom has passed down special pieces to me from her own collection." She told Melissa Massello, a journalist with Bentley University, "I was that girl who was called bossy."

On a trip to Kenya at age sixteen, Honegger was struck when she saw abject poverty for the first time. For two years after college, she volunteered with Food for the Hungry in Bolivia and Guatemala. In both countries, she saw that when people could generate even a small income, they could improve their and their families' futures. Several years later—then married with two children—Honegger began dreaming of combining her love of beautiful things, her knack for business, and her care for vulnerable people.

"I'm a capitalist; I call it 'compassionate capitalism,'" Honegger told Shellnutt. "There are really talented people living in resource-poor areas of the world, and all they need is access to a marketplace. And I'm going to start something for them."

Her dream took off in 2010. That year, Honegger visited a friend in Uganda and met Jalia and Daniel, two paper-bead necklace designers. They asked Jessica to sell some of their surplus back in the States. At the time, Honegger and her husband, Joe, felt called to adopt a child from Rwanda. So Honegger hosted a trunk show

in her home, featuring Jalia and Daniel's jewelry. The show attracted sixty people and garnered over four thousand dollars. Soon, other women approached Honegger to host their own parties. When sales exceeded her and her husband's ability to keep up, she partnered with friend Travis Wilson (MBA, Wharton).

Noonday Collection's aesthetic is eclectic, floral, and colorful, which is what you'd expect from jewelry made all over the globe. It's not unlike another BAM of sorts, Ten Thousand Villages, the national store chain founded by the Mennonite Central Committee in 1997. However, Noonday sells through individual women, called "ambassadors," who host trunk shows and earn a 20 to 25 percent commission. Honegger says ambassadors are the "driving force of the business" and glean business acumen from their experience.

"Our ambassadors are extremely motivated by issues of justice," Honegger told Shellnutt. "They enjoy women. They are looking for a way to not just give money to an organization but to be an active part of building a flourishing world." She said most of the ambassadors are working moms who want to earn extra income, set their own schedule, and feel like they are joining a bigger mission. They are tapping into the goodness of industry even while working mostly from home.

Likewise, Noonday's central office in Austin, Texas, is majority-women. Honegger says she is intentional about addressing the "confidence gap" among female leaders. "We encourage all of our team members to

participate in providing input and making decisions," she told Massello. "We have a majority of women in all decision-making roles, so our team learns by example."

Honegger says she knew that "the whole woman leading, working, business can have some baggage" in Christian communities. "It's been a hard road," she told Shellnutt. "I definitely struggled with balance and guilt and shame. But so much of it was having a real confidence in who God made me to be and what he created me to do."

In the process of realizing her dream, Honegger has been empowering women worldwide to discover a similar confidence: to manage a business, provide for their families, and taste firsthand the goodness of working "with willing hands" (Prov. 31:13) to add a bit more beauty to the world.

CHAPTER FIVE

You Are Female, And It Is Good

I am a child of the 1980s. This means there's a sizable collection of home videos devoted to my childhood. There's the video of my brother and me running in the backyard on Easter Day, scouting eggs and candy. (I'm the lanky one in glasses, standing three inches in front of the camera. You can't miss me.) There are piano recitals, Girl and Boy Scout ceremonies, and Thanksgiving dinners where everyone seems on the verge of sleep. In one video that my family and I watch every year, Tyler and I dance in our living room to a funky Peter Gabriel hit. It goes on longer than anyone expects, and Tyler's toddler feet slow to a sluggish pace. When the song ends, he turns to the camera and exclaims, "I'm pooped!" It's so adorable, I resent all over again that he diverted my parents' attention when he came into the world in December 1988.

There are home videos from further back, when we lived in Monterey, California, where my dad was serving in the Marine Corps. I don't know whether the memories precede the home videos or the videos gave me the memories. But Monterey is the setting of my earliest recollections. It is also the place where I first grew aware, dimly, that I was—am—a girl. I understood that playing the mom during "house" and meeting my first "boyfriend" were expressions of this.

Blessedly, my girlhood was mostly a *childhood*. I wasn't made to wear cumbersome, frilly dresses or to play with dolls. I had Barbies, yes, and I liked playing dress-up. But I was just as excited to play with an electric keyboard or a basketball. One home video follows our family to a nearby park. I am wearing a cotton sundress and Keds that were yellowed from being in the dusty earth of central California. A dress and dirty shoes—that about sums it up.

On the path from childhood to adulthood, something happens to all of us. Aided by waves of hormones (as well as awkward conversations about and with the opposite sex), when we are old enough to become self-aware, we necessarily become aware of being male or female. We notice our sex—the biological marks of maleness or femaleness—and we learn, by culture, what it will mean to live as male or female.[21] The Genesis account we explored in Chapter 3 tells us that maleness and femaleness are good, intended by God to glorify him as we live out the cultural mandate.

---

21. It should be noted that some people—an estimated .3 percent of the U.S. population—report experiencing, from an early age, a mismatch between their biological sex and corresponding gender; thus, they do not easily identify clearly as male or female. More theological resources are needed to understand persons who identify as transgender or who experience "gender dysphoria"—a clinical term for the experience of distress over a mismatch between one's sex and one's gender—and more pastoral responses are needed to reaffirm that, regardless of how well gender and biological sex correspond, all persons bear the image of God and are formed by him in a mother's womb (Ps. 139).

But do we, women, really believe that femaleness is a gift? Do we experience it as a core part of ourselves to express freely at the job as much as at home or church?

In an effort to gain footing in the world that culture has made—a world that is overwhelmingly built by men—some of us have tried to be *like* men. We have downplayed our femininity in order to fit in, to gain respect or a hearing, to lead a team. We have looked at our colleagues and tried to ape their manner and communication style. We have hidden our bodies under thick trouser suits and shoulder pads. We have denigrated other women for being too girly, too emotional, too tepid. I know I have.

But when we try to hide such a core part of our personhood, we are only one of the many people who lose out.

We have established that we bear the image of a Worker God and are thus called and invited to work, to have dominion over the works of God's hands, as Psalm 8 tell us. What if our femininity is intended not to hinder that call but to enrich it? What if our neighbors and institutions and churches need women *as women* in order to thrive?

The Most Important Thing About You

One of the most cogent books I've read on these themes is *Made for More: An Invitation to Live in God's Image*, by Hannah Anderson. As the Virginia writer and mother of three beautifully expresses, that we humans bear the image of God is the most important thing about us. Our image bearing is what distinguishes us from the rest of creation and all the heavenly beings. It is what crowns us with "glory and honor," to come back to Psalm 8. It's what enables us to know right from wrong. It's what establishes our capacity to be in intimate relationship with God our Maker.

As Anderson writes:

> *Imago Dei* means that your life has purpose and meaning because God has made you to be like Himself. *Imago Dei* means that your life has intrinsic value, not simply because of who you are as an individual, but because of who He is as your God. *Imago Dei* means that your life is sacred because He has stamped His identity upon yours.[22]

Our *Imago Dei* is the beginning and end of our identity. We live into that gift as male and female who together bear God's image (Gen. 1:27). Our sexual distinction—as well as the expression of it in a particular time, place, and culture—is a gift not only because it allows us to make more image bearers. Before Genesis speaks of Adam and Eve's progeny, it speaks of Adam and Eve's one-flesh union. Our maleness or femaleness is a gift because it grounds our relationship with people who are like us— more like us than any other thing in the world, in fact— yet profoundly other. "We are created in God's image for fellowship with God, and created male and female to be

---

22. Anderson, Hannah. *Made for More: An Invitation to Live in God's Image* (Chicago: Moody Publishers, 2014), 33.

in relation to one another," writes theologian Cherith Fee Nordling.[23] Our Trinitarian God himself exists in relationship between persons who are intimately related yet wholly other. And so we who bear his image are made to be in intimate relationship.

Yet when Christian communities talk about women's identity, we seldom start with the *Imago Dei*. "Women don't think about themselves [as] this direct reflection of the image of God," Anderson told me in 2014 at the Gospel Coalition Women's Conference. "They don't think of themselves as an image bearer of God, directly. And it's startling to me how that changes everything about the way you navigate your life."

For most of our inherited history, women weren't thought to be full persons at all. And it's important to recount this history, to see how Christians have bought in to falsehoods rooted in Greek philosophy rather than the Hebrew Scriptures.

A Brief History Lesson

"The conception of woman as a misbegotten man is fundamental to the Western worldview," writes philosopher Nancy Tuana. "The belief that woman is less than man—less perfect, less evolved, less divine, less rational, less moral, less healthy—is more than simply bias. . . . It is part of our inherited metaphysics."

---

23. Nordling, Cherith Fee. "The Human Person in the Christian Story," in *The Cambridge Companion to Evangelical Theology* (Cambridge, U.K.: Cambridge University Press, 2007).

And now for a very brief history lesson! (Stay with me, it gets good.)

Early Greek mythology attributed the existence of discord and evil to women. Hesiod's *Works and Days* named Pandora as the first woman. In Homer's *Iliad*, "women are seldom depicted as anything but causes of jealousy and war, or as part of the booty, along with animals as slaves," notes one philosopher.[24] Such a description from Homer reflects practices in Greek culture, where girls were not formally educated except in home-keeping.

Both Plato and Aristotle, arguably the most foundational thinkers of the West, believed that the ideal human is male and that women are fallen or deformed males. In his creation story, *Timaeus,* Plato imagined a world in which all humans were male. Men who used their intellect to conquer their "passions" (emotions and sensations) would be blessed in the life after death. Men who failed to overcome their passions would be reincarnated as women.

Aristotle saw a natural hierarchy in the created order based on each created thing's function. It was self-evident to him that the Greek polis would be governed by the rational principles of men. To Aristotle, the ideal Greek home was one in which the slave fulfilled his or her natural function by providing food, and the woman fulfilled her natural function by bearing children. Both Aristotle and Plato envisioned the soul—the locus of reason, intellect, and perception of spiritual and moral truth—as the arena of men. The

---

24. Moller Okin, Susan. *Women in Western Political Thought* (Princeton, NJ: Princeton University Press, 1979).

body—the realm of passions, appetites, as well as decay and death—belonged to women.

Aristotle, in particular, emphasized that the differences in male and female bodies indicated a fundamental difference in male and female social and political roles. He distinguished between the family (private sphere) and the state (public sphere) and saw in men's and women's natures a correlation—men belonged to the state; women, to the family.

The Christians came along and kind of made all this worse. To be sure, some early theologians diverged from Aristotle and Plato in key ways. Foremost, they rejected the body/soul divide that marked Platonic philosophy, instead proclaiming the radical notion that God himself took on flesh and redeemed the human body for eternity in the Resurrection. Unfortunately, other major theologians took the view that women are inferior to men—reflected in both belief and practice in their time—and confirmed it with certain interpretations of Scripture.

Augustine of Hippo, the most important Western theologian, did teach that women had souls and were included in God's redemption in Christ. But only when she is "together with her husband" does she bear the image of God. "When she is referred separately to her quality of *help-meet*, which regards the woman herself alone, then she is not the image of God; but as regards the man alone, he is the image of God as fully and completely as when the woman too is joined with him in one."[25] Augustine also

---

25. Schaff, Philip, and Henry Wace, eds. "On the Trinity," in *A Select Library of Nicene and Post-Nicene Fathers of the Christian Church* (Charleston, SC: Nabu Press, 2010).

took Paul's teachings on head coverings and connected them to women's naturally weak minds: "Have women not this renewal of the mind in which is the image of God? Who would say this? But in the sex of their body they [women] do not signify this [mind]; therefore they are bidden to be veiled."

Women's weak minds were one reason Augustine and other theologians believed women were ill suited for any role in which they could rule or legislate. Eve, the first woman, clearly couldn't discern good from evil, as she was tricked by the serpent. "For the woman taught the man once, and made him guilty of disobedience, and wrought our ruin," wrote John Chrysostom, archbishop of Constantinople (397–407 A.D.) "Therefore because she made bad use of her power over the man, or rather her equality with him, God made her subject to her husband."

Many centuries later, reformer Martin Luther picked up on this theme by teaching that women were to be excluded from politics as punishment for Eve's rebellion. "She herself would also have been a partner in the rule which is now entirely the concern of males. . . . However, they cannot perform the functions of men, teach, rule, etc." John Calvin wrote that women were created in the image of God "in the second degree"; similarly, Luther taught that Eve was akin to Adam as the moon is akin to the sun: "a more beautiful work God, nevertheless . . . not the equal of the male in glory and prestige."

In the eighteenth and nineteenth centuries, outside the church, scientists would "prove" the natural barring of women from any work in the public realm. It was believed that women would be psychologically and physically harmed if they tried to compete with men in the workforce. One scientist warned that "monotony, depression, bodily fatigue, and 'constrained position'" of industrial work would bring irreparable harm to women. Apparently, he had not consulted a woman on what it's like to care for small children.

In her brilliant essay "The Human-Not-Quite-Human," essayist and novelist Dorothy Sayers pinpoints the effect of millennia of such teaching and beliefs: In sum, we have inherited a view that women are vastly different from all other humans because they are first and last women. "*Vir* is male and *Femina* is female; but *Homo* is male and female," Sayers observes, restating the plain truth of Genesis 1:27. And yet "Man is always dealt with as both *Homo* and *Vir,* but Women only as *Femina*." In other words, when men do things, a human explanation is given, but when women do things, a female explanation is given. Before we think of women as human, we think of them as women.

Sayers recounts a newspaper article reporting that bus passengers like to ride on the side of the bus closest to the curb. Men do this because they find it more physically comfortable; women, because they want to look at the shopwindows. Women care only about clothing (a female concern), not physical comfort (a human concern), you see.

She goes on to imagine what it would be like for men to be treated with this condescension. "He would be edified by solemn discussions about 'Should Men Serve in Drapery

Establishments?' and acrimonious ones about 'Tea-Drinking Men'; by cross-shots of public affairs 'from the masculine angle' . . . and at dinner-parties he would hear the whee-dling, unctuous, predatory female voice demand: 'And why should you trouble your handsome little head about poli-tics?'" Some seventy years later, Sayers's satire is both sting-ing and sobering.

The Womanhood Crunch

Of course, all Christians today affirm that women are human, full stop. We can be grateful that, regardless of how they read Scripture, our leaders and theologians affirm that women fully bear the image of God and thus receive the same measure of dignity, worth, and blessing conferred upon men.

Despite this bedrock truth, we are prone to treat women as this other kind of human, a category of person wholly unique in gifts, dispositions, and essence. It's no wonder that many Christian women are tired of this sugges-tion; as Sayers writes, "What is repugnant to every human being is to be reckoned always as a member of a class and not as an individual person."

In many Christian communities, we slot women into roles—as supporters or helpers, as people who find their identity only *through* or *next to* other people. Or we identify women with certain virtues—like gentleness or peace—even though Scripture doesn't dole out the fruits of the Spirit along gender lines (Gal. 5:22). Some Christian com-munities think of womanhood primarily in terms of physical appearance, emphasizing modesty and simple dress. Others locate all women's identity in a universal motherhood where women's decisions and actions always arise from maternal "life giving." (I had a writer friend once suggest that, as a woman editor, I give life to people by leading a Christian magazine. I doubt she would say this if she saw all the red lines in the articles I edit.)

In other words, we make femaleness sound like a to-do list rather than a gift from a mysterious, surprising, and endlessly creative God. This is too bad, because it makes us look more concerned with gender roles than Our Father is.

I met godly, virtuous women who are their best, fullest selves when they are leading a company, making business decisions, and planning strategic initiatives. I met Christian women who are in their vocational sweet spot when they are presiding over state supreme court rulings and managing multimillion-dollar mutual funds. (More on these two later.) I met faithful Christian women who are devoted mothers and are deeply content managing the home and supporting their husband's career. I know a lot of women who are gentle and peaceful and love serving others; we all could learn a lot from them.

But the fact that I need to assure readers of this underscores our collective fear that femaleness could be multifaceted and thus messy. Whereas women contain within themselves enough complexity to be both strong and weak, assertive and yielding, nurturing one minute and directive the next, we want them to choose one way of bearing the image of God.

I believe such desires arise, understandably, from a fear

that our culture wants to write off maleness and femaleness as mere social constructs. Gender norms have changed rapidly in the past half century, even within the past five years. It's no coincidence that calls to uphold biblical womanhood arose soon after second-wave feminism had gained cultural footing. As ministry leader Nancy Leigh DeMoss writes, "The feminist revolution was supposed to bring women greater fulfillment and freedom. But I can't help feeling a sense of sadness over what has been forfeited in the midst of the upheaval—namely, the beauty, the wonder, and the treasure of the distinctive makeup of women." Because Scripture calls "male and female" good, many Christians believe that lawmakers and activists and media pundits are trying to take away a gift, that we will lose something meant to be a blessing.

But I wonder if many Christians have erred in equal and opposite proportion to this outside threat. If mainstream culture reduces femaleness to a construct, church culture loads femaleness with a "universal essence" not actually described in Scripture. If mainstream culture thinks gender roles are unimportant, church culture makes them too important. As Anderson notes:

> Gender is too important . . . it's part of the way the world is shaped, but it's not the only thing shaping it. Women don't know how to think of themselves as people; they think of themselves as women. It's fueled in the church in how we talk about women.

And how do we in the church talk about women?
As disciples who need to be matured in the faith in a

way utterly unique from all the other (male) disciples. In other words—to paraphrase Sayers—Christian women are the "disciple-not-quite-disciple." They are humans, of course, but a very special "other" or "opposite" type of disciple who needs to be treated in feminine ways or with feminine teaching.

One concrete example: how we do conferences. (Conferences are to Western evangelicals what the Eucharist is to Catholics.) Every year, events like Catalyst, Q, Story, and the Justice Conference draw thousands of Christians to hear biblical teaching, engage in cultural issues of the day, and receive practical tools for making an impact for Christ. These are all relatively neutral interests and tools, applicable to men and women alike. Yet they feature mostly male speakers, often in alarming imbalance. Men can speak on general topics, but women can speak only on women's topics.

The Nines, a digital conference hosted by Leadership Network—which officially supports women in church leadership—drew ire in 2013 for designing a lineup of 110 speakers that featured four women. Journalist Jonathan Merritt went on to tally the gender breakdown of other popular conferences' speakers. Even organizations that are neutral on or support women's leadership struggled mightily to achieve gender parity, with four of five speakers on average being men.[26] To be sure, speaker lineups often come from personal connections, and men in ministry tend to be

26. Merritt, Jonathan. "Are Christian Conferences Sexist?: *Religion News Service,* November 13, 2013, http://jonathanmerritt.religionnews.com/2013/11/13/christian-conferences-sexist-nines-controversy-prompts-reflection/.

friends with other men in ministry. And we could attribute the lack of women experts to unfair gender biases in every professional sector and facet of church life. Regardless, such an imbalance can communicate, however unintentionally, that the core of the Christian life is both led and lived out by men, while women do their "Christian women" activities on the edges.

Meanwhile, women's conferences pick up where such national conferences leave off. The IF:Gathering, founded by Bible teacher Jennie Allen in 2013, is intended to "gather, equip, and unleash" women to live purposefully for Christ. In its first year, it attracted twelve hundred women and at least forty thousand more who tuned in to the live simulcast. This signals that Christian women are famished for discipleship and ministry empowerment. LifeWay Women, a branch of the Southern Baptist Convention's publishing and research arm, hosts events and simulcasts providing teachings from Beth Moore and Priscilla Shirer. And since 2012, the Gospel Coalition has hosted a biennial women's conference that provides Bible study, theological training, and relational support for some four thousand women from thirty-eight countries, according to numbers from its 2014 gathering.

Even still, dividing out conferences in this way can subtly suggest that women need a particular type of Christian discipleship because women are very particular types of Christians, radically different in their spiritual needs than male Christians.

The effect is the same when publishers market Bibles on one hand and women's Bibles on the other; when church websites run photos of groups of men to advertise activities meant for men and women alike; and when certain Christian magazines launch women's sites to cover topics that touch all people.[27] Yet when we turn to Scripture itself, we find femaleness—originally intended to be a gift rather than a hindrance—wonderfully restored to something a bit less pink and a bit more human.

Jesus and the Women

When I studied art history in college, I looked at a lot of paintings, usually reproduced on slides and projected on a white screen or wall. The classroom setting didn't really foster a spirit of contemplation. But a handful of paintings from the currents of history can be so powerful that before you have a chance to interpret them, they interpret you.

In one such painting, a young dark-haired woman draped in the folds of a brown robe sits on the edge of a bed. Her hands are clasped. The room is lit only by a shaft of light that hovers to her left. The light seems to gaze at the woman, waiting. The woman has tilted her head toward the light. Is she pleased? Disturbed? Overwhelmed? That we can't tell only adds to the intrigue of the painting.

---

27. A colleague and I launched Her.meneutics, *Christianity Today*'s women's site, in 2009. The express intent was to elevate women's voices, which have sometimes been faint or absent in evangelical institutions. Some readers have questioned why we didn't just have more women writing for *Christianity Today*. The magazine, after all, is meant for the whole body of Christ. After six years in operation, I can say that Her.meneutics has managed to do both: It has carved out a space for women to discuss cultural and theological issues, *and* it has become a gateway for more women to write for the print magazine. A parallel would be if the Catalyst conference created a women's track in which workshops were led by women—who also spoke from the main stage.

Its title—*The Annunciation*—gives us a clue. It is one of the many from nineteenth-century realist painter Henry Ossawa Tanner, who once said to his father, a prominent bishop in the African Methodist Episcopal Church, "You preach from the pulpit, and I will preach with my brush." Tanner eschewed the abstract and often jarring expressionism of his artistic peers to capture what he called a "universal humanity." *The Annunciation* (1898) is part of a series of biblical themes that Tanner explored after visiting the Holy Land. For the past two thousand years, most painters have cast biblical figures and scenes in ethereal light, halos, and cherubic expressions. But Tanner stripped the biblical figures of their otherworldly glow and brought them down to a flesh-and-blood earth. One Philadelphia art critic notes that Tanner "desanctified" the figures of Scripture. I tend to think he "rehumanized" the sacredness of those figures.

Tanner's treatment of Mary the God Bearer (*theotokos*) is a helpful aide as women consider what it means to work unto the Lord as image bearers. What I love most about *The Annunciation* is the way it replaces Mary the icon with Mary the human—one who could "stand on her soul's own two feet" before God, to paraphrase writer Sarah Bessey. Instead of coming face-to-face with the idealized woman, who symbolizes a particular womanly piety, we see a vulnerable woman meant to symbolize the frailty and smallness of *all people* before the living God. Here, as in other artistic renderings of Mary, a woman takes the posture befitting all humans: the "yes" to God's will to redeem his people.

Of course, Mary was no generic human. Her ability to

bear children was central to her response to God's call. But in a way that only God can, he incorporates the very thing that would have restricted Mary's social standing and cultural influence—her womanhood—and made it central to her participation in his work. That is what the Son of God, "born of a woman," did in all his interactions with women, healing and teaching them even as he called them to repentance.

The Scriptures are replete with examples of Jesus interacting with women in radically direct ways that scandalized his peers. When a woman considered defiled due to a twelve-year flow of blood touches Jesus' garment in the crowd, he heals her, removing her shame and calling her "daughter." When the woman at the well says she has no husband, Jesus engages her in a long theological discourse about worship, making her the first evangelist to the Samaritans. When Mary and Martha of Bethany fight over housework while hosting an important man in their home, Jesus praises Mary for sitting at his feet to learn—a person made to know and love her Creator and Redeemer *directly*. And in a striking detail found in all four Gospels, women are the first to receive the earth-shattering news that Jesus is no longer in the tomb. They are the first people in all the world to find the tomb of Jesus empty.

None of this means that Christ came to strip women of their womanhood, to make his followers, female or male, generically human. Galatians 3:28—"There is neither Jew nor Gentile, neither slave nor free, nor is there male and female, for you are all one in Christ Jesus"—remains among the most debated biblical passages. But scholars of all stripes agree that it doesn't mean Christ came to *erase* gender distinction. Rather, it means that in Christ, gender no longer determines who's in and who's out of the newly formed gospel family, whose *Imago Dei* shines ever and ever brighter as Christ restores us to our right relationship with God and others. The only factor for becoming a member of God's family is believing in his Son. And the Son has invited women to himself.

Not an Accident

All of this is good news for women discerning how to bear the image of God in their professional lives.

It means, foundationally, that you are "God's handiwork, created in Christ Jesus to do good works, which God prepared in advance for us to do" (Eph. 2:10). In Christ, you are saved by grace, through faith, to love and serve him in all parts of life—and not just the spiritual parts such as worship and missions. As Mark D. Roberts, executive director of the Max De Pree Center for Leadership at Fuller Theological Seminary, notes, "The good works of [Ephesians 2] Verse 10 are not obviously religious activities scattered throughout an otherwise secular life. Rather, the good works encompass the whole of the Christian, all that we do by God's grace for God's purposes."

Your being a woman and not a man will necessarily come to bear on *how* you enact these good works in the professional sphere, as in any other sphere. Your femaleness is not an accident; it is not a liability. It is a real and good part of who you are, a direct imaging of God. Speaking in the broadest of generalities, it will probably (though not necessarily!) make you sensitive to the needs and experiences of other people. It probably means that the right and left hemispheres of your brain are more interconnected than in the brain of the dude in the next cubicle over. Go ahead, ladies, celebrate your hemispheric hyperconnectivity.

But don't think that because you love solving math problems or fixing the electrical wiring in your home, you are no longer doing good works in a manner that pleases Christ. In my interviews with groups of women, I certainly observed general trends in occupation. There were more professors and teachers than there were engineers. I met a lot of writers and no wrestlers. Many of the women performed work that somehow benefited children, such as children in foster care or in the public school system. However, such observable trends hardly illuminate an occupational path for all women at all times.

Before she was nominated to the U.S. Court of Appeals for the Fifth Circuit, Priscilla Owen was a member of the Texas Supreme Court. Today, she presides over cases involving everything from the death penalty to the Internal Revenue Service, from abortion to arbitration. When our group asked whether there were observable trends along gender lines among the seventeen judges, Owen noted that "men can write just as passionately" about "women's issues." She doesn't feel discriminated against as one of the six women on the court. "When you are one among many on an appellate court such as ours, there is just no question that each of us has the authority and the power," she said. "It's the office itself, not what your personality brings to it."

Similarly, Helen Young Hayes, whom I met at a gathering in Denver, established her authority and power through a knack for managing stocks. After receiving a degree in economics from Yale University, she worked for twenty-one years on Wall Street, eventually managing the global and international business side of Janus Worldwide Fund in the 1990s. At one point she was responsible for managing over $50 billion in stock portfolios. Hayes retired in 2003, in part because she and her husband adopted a fifth child; in part because her husband was diagnosed that year with a life-threatening illness and needed much care. The daughter of Chinese immigrants, Hayes told *FullFill* magazine, "In the world of stock analysts in the 1980s and 1990s there were few women and few minorities. My mentors were all men. But they always believed I could accomplish more than I thought I could." Today, Hayes's name is synonymous with Janus's glory days.

For these and other women, femaleness doesn't dictate *what* they do for work. Rather, it adds one more dazzling dimension to *how* they do that work.

Ruth Abaya knew from an early age that she wanted to be a doctor. A native of Nigeria, Abaya spent much of her childhood in Toledo, Ohio, while her parents both worked toward doctorates. Now she is a pediatric emergency medicine doctor in the Philadelphia area, where, she says, "a lot of my mentors have been women." Abaya believes that her department chair and her medical director, both women, exhibit a positive work/life balance and ways of connecting with patients and families. Abaya herself chose to research gun violence as part of her ER work, she said,

> based on a maternal response to a seventeen-year-old kid in the adult trauma bay who was losing his liver and his kidney because they had been shot up. He was an otherwise totally healthy kid. And I had a very maternal moment with him because his mom wasn't there. And that's not to say that a male couldn't have had a paternal moment, but I can't imagine that because I'm not a man. I experienced it as a woman, and I was grateful to do so.

Similarly, Jenna Henderson says the mission of A Rocha Nashville—a chapter of a global conservation program founded by Christians in 1983—is enhanced because she is leading as a mother and not, say, a professional scientist or theologian. She believes her approach is "communal and holistic," in that the program's education takes place in neighborhoods, in backyards, and over meals that engage children and adults alike. "In general, it means that the work becomes more of a household activity than a professional endeavor," says the mother of two. Under the leadership of singer-songwriter Sandra McCracken, the work of A Rocha Nashville also incorporates reflection on the Creator and Creation through hymns old and new. Other women musicians such as Jill Phillips, Sarah Masen, and Sara Groves have contributed to A Rocha's musical body. "Being a part-time working mom can feel like an impediment,

[with] lack of time and focus," she told me. "But maybe it's a blessing for it to have to be so integrated with people and life."

My friend Kate, the business leader mentioned in Chapter 3, says it took a while in her career to see the value added of leading "as a woman" and simply herself. Early on, she says, she thought she needed to be "like a man" to succeed or to come across as professional. Over time, she grew more comfortable bringing her authentic self to her leadership. "I primarily lead through emotion and intuition," she says. "I often have a gut sense of the right decision or of an impending problem. . . . I've learned to pay attention to those feelings and emotional insights . . . to translate those hunches into logical arguments that I can lay out to my boss or coworkers."

Pam, the psychologist/massage therapist, also from Chapter 3, sees her femaleness as a direct advantage in her work. She notes that most "touch" in modern Western society has been sexualized—"especially if offered by a male," she says, given our pop-culture tropes about "creepy dudes." "The work I do is often more easily received because I am a woman," says Pam. "I am proud to have the opportunity to embody this aspect of God's love, care, and healing," something she can embody precisely because she is a woman.

To be sure, in many lines of work, there are only good and bad—not male and female—ways of doing it. In her talk "Are Women Human?," given to a British women's society in 1938, Dorothy Sayers lamented getting requests from magazine editors and "congenital imbeciles" (her words) to speak on writing detective novels "from the woman's point of view." She scoffed at the idea: "You might as well ask what is the female angle on an equilateral triangle." In other words, a detective novel is either riveting and well constructed or not. For many types of work, gender will have virtually no effect.

Most days, I think of editing a magazine in this way. There are many ways to make a magazine article compelling, clear, and timely. But in spite of the ongoing wars between the AP adherents and the *Chicago Manual of Style* circles, good editing is rooted in good writing, which follows the rules of proper grammar and style. As far I can tell, I don't edit with a feminine touch. I don't keep a schedule, respond to emails, or read the news in a way that's fundamentally different from that of male colleagues. I've thought about my male colleagues: Do they "exercise dominion" over dangling modifiers and factual errors? I've concluded that any insistence that men and I do our jobs as editors in fundamentally different ways comes down to semantics. I imagine the same is true for physicists, nurses, baristas, and brokers.

Then a friend shared with me that I had been one of the first editors to accept her unsolicited pitch and work intently with her to improve and publish it. Her work for *CT* magazine has opened a multitude of writing and speaking doors. "You have been a mentor to me and to many other women," she told me. "Your in-depth response to my pitch a few years ago gave me confidence to keep developing my writing." I have to think that our editor/writer relationship is possible in part because I identify and empathize with her as a woman. Something in her writer's voice, in her experiences, in her outlook on the world, resonates with me in an undeniably gendered way.

We don't—and indeed can't—turn off our femaleness when we walk into the office or classroom; when we try to, we can end up seeming sexist, as if working like a woman is a liability or source of shame. Rather, we can work *with* our gender, letting it inform but never overwhelm our particular tasks and decisions. It's like one blossom in the bouquet of our identity.

Okay, that metaphor was way too girly for me. Here's another: It's like one driver in the set of clubs we use to finish the course. Either way, your gender is a gift and not an accident, and also not the most important thing about you. Now go figure our what God wants you to do with it.

Elyse Bealer

When Elyse Bealer was seven years old, two things happened that would set her life course. First, she participated in a school science fair and got hooked. "That was the first time I had gone through the scientific method," she said. "I was fascinated by doing experiments, learning, seeing what happens." Bealer would go on to consistently win first, second, or third place in district science fairs up through eighth grade, and in 2006, she earned a bachelor's of science, chemical and biomolecular engineering from Houston's Rice University.

Second, seven-year-old Bealer watched her grandmother—a member of the Cherokee Nation, one of the largest Native American tribes—suffer the first of several heart attacks and strokes. She had taught Bealer the customs, dances, and language belonging to her Cherokee heritage, and her own great-great-grandmother had survived the infamous Trail of Tears from North Carolina to Oklahoma. As Bealer made hospital visits to see her grandmother, she learned about the paltry health care in many Native American communities. Her grandmother later suffered from a stroke, diabetes, cancer, and Alzheimer's before passing away in 2006.

That year, Bealer says, she had a choice: She could join Teach for America, move to South Dakota,

and educate Lakota children; or she could accept a job at Merck, a Fortune 100 company and one of the largest pharmaceutical purveyors in the world, with $42.2 billion in sales in 2014 alone.

Nearly a decade later, Bealer serves fellow Native Americans—and not through Teach for America. She worked her way up through Merck's ranks, eventually chairing an internal business roundtable for Native American and indigenous employees. Today, alongside leading Merck's leadership development program, Bealer coleads Project Sacred Dream, a business center owned by the Cheyenne River Sioux Tribe in Eagle Butte, South Dakota. There, 86 percent of tribe members are unemployed. "The number one way to address health care disparities in Native American populations is not giving away medication . . . it's alleviating poverty," says Bealer. "And the number one way that Merck could help Indian Country is to give them jobs." The business center—one of the first in the United States owned by a minority—is set up to eventually employ five hundred members of Cheyenne and other nearby tribes.

For Project Sacred Dream, Bealer was honored by the National Center for American Indian Enterprise Development with the "Native American 40 Under 40" award in 2013. She also serves in the Society for Women Engineers (SWE), an organization she joined in college. "Having that positive interaction with science when I was young, I never remember thinking, *Girls can do that* or *That's a nerdy, geeky thing.*" She travels

to local fairs and gives special awards to girls. "It's an award to encourage them to keep going."

Bealer, married to a financial adviser for Merrill Lynch, intends to encourage her own daughter in a similar way. Having children, she says, "has probably increased my desire for meaningful work. . . . It reinforces my sense of purpose. I feel this greater responsibility to do something impactful with my life." While she says it's been more difficult to return to Merck after having her son, she wants to model for her daughter the dual calls to career and family. "I'm sure there will be things she wants me to be there for, and I'll miss it. But ultimately, it's important that my kids know what I do during the day, why I choose not to be home with them all day, every day."

Like many other women interviewed for this book, Bealer says that working full-time while raising children wouldn't be possible without a husband who's "a hundred and fifty percent supportive of me thriving outside the home." This means sharing cooking, cleaning, and child care. The family's choices haven't always been accepted by her church community; in a small group for parents of young children, she found herself better able to connect with the men than with the women. The other moms would organize get-togethers during the day. "I've spent a lot of my life feeling like some kind of alien," says Elyse.

But she draws confidence from believing that her mission at Merck ultimately comes from God and the

faith that she came to at age fourteen during summer camp. "Being a Native American and a Christian, both are core pieces of my identity. . . . Meaningful work means bringing my whole self to work," says Bealer. "God has been the centerpiece of opening and closing doors for me."

CHAPTER SIX

How She Does It All

As one of the women in the Austin group started to tear up, I inwardly glowed. I know, it sounds horrible. But journalists always hope that someone will cry during an interview; it means you are hitting on bedrock human experience. When another woman in the group started to cry, I knew I had hit journalistic gold.

The first woman, Chelsea Brown (now Lam), was working at the Texas Capitol for a state senator involved in pro-life legislation. The group of about fifteen women had chatted for several minutes about working outside the home and raising children at the same time. Then Chelsea, twenty-four at the time, shyly spoke up. She admitted that, as prestigious as her job was, she was far more drawn to the work her friend is doing: raising and homeschooling her children. "It's one of the first pictures I've seen where I've said, 'This is an area where I could bring my intelligence, my care, my desire to be a mom spiritually,'" said Chelsea. And she experienced some shame over this desire: "If I do that, it's not enough. It's this crazy Proverbs Thirty-one pressure, that I'm not an accomplished professional woman."

After several minutes of discussion, Tish Harrison Warren, an ordained Anglican priest with two children, also started crying. Working outside the home was something, in her very makeup, that she couldn't *not* do—and that brought some shame. "I so wish I were content with just being at home, in terms of *simply* being at home," she said. "There are people who have these preternatural spiritual gifts of mothering, and I don't have them. And that's hard because I love my children so much, and I feel that they suffer because they have a mom who has these other gifts, and I'm still trying to figure out what they are. But they are not mothering very small children."

These moments in the conversation were powerful. They revealed how motherhood—perhaps more than any other type of work a woman can take up—affects all the other work she might do, all the other callings she might pursue. Based on the group conversations I've had over the past year, I have learned that having children shapes women's bodies (literally), schedules, political views, self-identity, spirituality, relationships, and professional choices. Sometimes motherhood presents itself as a question mark that hangs over a person's life as she pursues other good work. Sometimes it's a period that halts other callings and pursuits full-stop. Sometimes it's an exclamation point, a gift of grace that energizes all other endeavors.

This is not to say that motherhood itself stands at the center of women's work. Amid pronouncements that motherhood, marriage, and home management are the "central, core, dominant commitments of a woman's life,"[28] most women I spoke with saw their mothering in tandem with, not trumping, other good work. Even the women I met who were full-time stay-at-home moms—and there were only eight out of 125—saw motherhood as important, but not the only work they were supposed to be doing when their kids were little. To be sure, the women who came to the group conversations probably came because they *do* work professionally; some of them had stayed at home to raise kids for a season. So we can't extrapolate from these groups out into the church and beyond. Still, I was surprised that of all the Christian moms I met, very few were pursuing motherhood solely.

If we define the stay-at-home mom as the Census Bureau does—someone who opts out of the labor force for at least a year expressly to raise children and manage a household—then the full-time stay-at-home mom is an increasingly rare breed, with 71 percent of all American moms today doing paid work.[29]

That said, the *prospect* of motherhood weighs significantly on most women's professional aspirations and identities. We could attribute this to biology and its ticking clock (an expression I've long disliked; a womb is not a bomb). We could attribute it to spiritual design and God's command to be fruitful and multiply. We could attribute it to

28. Piper, John. "Honoring the Biblical Call of Motherhood," *Desiring God*, May 8, 2005, http://www.desiringgod.org/messages/honoring-the-biblical-call-of-motherhood.

29. "7 Key Findings About Stay-at-Home Moms," Pew Research Center, April 8, 2014.

strong social pressure and norms, from our parents or our peers or pop culture, for the notion of having children as normative. Whatever the cause, it is the case that most women who *can* choose whether to have children weigh the choice seriously.

Something's Gotta Give

"You can have it all—just not at the same time."

In Chapter 4, we reviewed how work life and home life were fairly seamless for most of human history. That in the past three hundred years, industrialization took work away from the home—and in the past seventy-five, many women began to realize they wanted careers as much as men did. We are now in an era when many women are trying to bring work and home back together after they have been ripped apart. The task is Herculean—or perhaps Xena-like, or whoever the female Hercules is.

I say "women" and not "people" here because the truth is that many men *can* have it all at the same time. I know, I know, all you male readers are thinking of your mounting stress levels, how you feel consistently pulled between duties at the office and duties at home. The struggle is real, in the way that limitations on time and energy are real and genderless, and in the way that many modern workplaces are ill prepared to support workers in the decision to have families.

Yet in another way, the conversation about work/life balance is unique to women. Think about it: Have you ever heard of a man being quietly let go from the job because he and his wife had a baby? (In fact, some studies have found that men get a fatherhood bonus, a pay raise when a new baby arrives, regardless of performance.) Have you heard a man post on Facebook that he is "so blessed!" that his wife lets him get out of the house a few hours a week? A man praised for taking care of the kids, running a successful business, *and* managing to keep the house spotless? How does he do it all? I've heard plenty of men talk about wanting to be at home more, and men stressing about the mounting demands of work. But I've never heard men wonder aloud whether they can "have it all."

Meanwhile, women know that—unless you have attained Sheryl Sandbergian levels of wealth that allow you to hire other people for the tasks most parents do daily—something's gotta give. This is true especially for women, who continue to bear a majority of child-rearing and domestic duties during the infamous second shift, even while attaining more responsibilities and leadership at work. Balancing act, stretched, juggling, worn thin—this is the language of exhaustion many women use to describe their dilemma. For all the women I met, the idea of having it all seemed naive, privileged, and laughable.

After helping to host a women's event at Redeemer Presbyterian Church's Center for Faith at Work (CFW), I received an email from one of the attendees, a professional violist and writer in New York City with two children. She said that she had enjoyed the event and was grateful that CFW was hosting a discussion just for women. However, she observed, the conversation didn't adequately address motherhood.

I emailed her back in the most courteous tone I could muster that the two women leading the event (Katherine Leary Alsdorf and I) were not the best candidates to speak on motherhood, as neither of us is a mother. I also stated that I believe conversations about calling for Christian women too quickly go to motherhood.

The attendee clarified that she didn't mean motherhood itself was a woman's core vocation. Rather, motherhood informed most women's work in inescapable ways. She captured the quandary in poignant detail:

> It is very difficult to choose a career when the result is spending tens of thousands of dollars on child care a year and watching (or not watching) someone else parent and love your children more hours of the week than you do. Yet it is also very difficult to choose family when a woman has worked hard in the 30 years prior to build a career and a reputation and gain experience that taking time off to raise kids would jeopardize, at best. As you know, there's no job guarantee beyond the 3 months' maternity leave (only partially paid) in America, only very short paternity leave (if any), and yet America is filled to the brim with driven, intelligent, career-oriented women who also are or are becoming mothers.

Notice that first line: "It is very difficult to choose . . ." In other words, the multitude of *choices* now available to women—to get multiple advanced degrees; to pursue careers as CEOs and surgeons and senators; to spend a year traveling the world alone; to use birth control to have children (or not) at a "strategic" time; to start a business from home thanks to Web technology—bring anxiety even as they bring convenience and personal freedom. Our grandmothers might look at our lives and marvel at the choices available to us. At the same time, we might envy, on one level, the relative ease with which they made choices, as they simply had fewer of them.

To use a literary metaphor, most women of our grandmothers' generation had a relatively clear script to read from: Complete school, get married, have children, enjoy retired life and grandchildren, end scene. For women of our generation, the script reads more like a choose-your-own-adventure book—more exciting, perhaps, but also more likely that you can take a wrong turn and end up in a pit of quicksand.

We also aren't always prepped beforehand—by parents or schools or churches—to know how to make the right choices for ourselves and our families. As Bronwyn Lea, a writer and mother of three in California, put it: "I assumed I would have children and never gave any thought to who would take care of them. It was, 'I'll have children' as if that were like, 'Oh, I'll own a car.'"

Similarly, Halee Gray Scott, a scholar and author of the book *Dare Mighty Things: Mapping the Challenges of Leadership for Christian Women,* says, "We were the first generation that were told since we were three years old, 'You can do anything.'" As children of the 1970s, Scott and her peers grew up when women "had come a long way, baby." But two years into her Ph.D., she says, "it hit me like a sledgehammer in the face: *Oh my gosh, no. You can't do it all at the same time.*" Scott has since declined two tenure-track teaching positions, in part to stay home with her two children while continuing to write and speak on leadership. Through motherhood, "God has healed a lot of broken places in me," says Scott, who is confident that it was the right choice for her and her family. But thinking about those two tenure-track offers is "frightening," she says. "Is it ever going to come around again?"

That anxiety hangs like a cloud over many Christian women. According to a major 2014 survey conducted by Barna Group, only three out of every ten Christian moms say they are confident they are making the "right" choices for themselves and their families. Some 62 percent of Christian moms are dissatisfied with the proverbial work/life balance, which so often seems like choosing to feel guilty in two areas of life at once. And 34 percent of Christian moms say their church community does not provide much or any support as they face mounting choices and exhaustion.

To be sure, every person, male or female, with kids or not, faces barriers to doing the work they deeply desire in any given season. In the broader "having it all" conversation, one of the most common responses has been, "No one can have it all." After Anne-Marie Slaughter's incisive 2012 *Atlantic* cover story, James Joyner, a security-studies scholar raising two young children, wrote, "The fact is that life is full of trade-offs. It's not possible to 'have it all.' It never was. And never will be. For women or for men." Similarly, *Esquire* editor Richard Dorment reported that men report higher rates of work-life stress than women do. "Hearing Gail Collins grumble about changing the corporate mindset . . . or reading Slaughter complain that our society values hard work over family . . . makes me feel like channeling Tom Hanks in *A League of Their Own:* There's no crying in baseball." In other words, women, if you are unhappy with the choices you have to make now that you've arrived in the workplace, suck it up and welcome to adulthood, where no one gets everything he or she wants.

But when we say "having it all," we don't mean having everything we desire at any point in time, on a whim. Rather, we mean having a meaningful professional life and an invested family life at the same time. It's something that many men do take for granted.

As I spoke to Christian women about the challenges of pursuing a meaningful professional life and an invested family life simultaneously, I identified three barriers: *bodies, bosses,* and—yes, to keep the alliteration—the official *bureau of lady judgment.*

Bodies

We have given women the vote. We have created laws ensuring that women can't be fired simply for being women. We have fought for women to be paid as much as men for the same work. But for all our advancements in gender equality, we still haven't found a way to get a man to carry a child in his body. Or to make sure he throws up, swells up, and passes out at eight-thirty P.M. for nine months, at the same rates as women. When it comes to our campaigns for equality, biology seems retrograde and out of touch. And in many cases, it still gets the final word.

First, women who want to have children are constrained by a window of time that men are not (a fact that strikes many women as grossly unfair). Imagine that women could have kids at any age, and *poof*, the work/life balance quagmire vanishes. Or it at least recedes to the normal level of anxiety that comes with any human limitation. However, as biology would have it, the prime season in which a woman would try to have kids is also the prime season for professionally kicking butt and taking names.

This double bind forces a choice for many women: to work full-time, to work part-time, or to leave the workforce while having young kids. It's a choice with big consequences, not only for a woman's career but also for her identity formation. It's why, says Hannah Anderson, a woman typically faces identity upheaval in her twenties and thirties, while a man's stereotypically typically presents in midlife. (Note that the term "midlife crisis" almost always conjures a man.) Biology presses the question: "What kind of woman am I? What kind do I want to be?"

Further, women who desire to work professionally and have children at the same time face the *physicality* of parenting in a way that men don't and, indeed, can't. Anderson compares mothering three kids to "taking on a career of manual labor." Even many manual laborers can bank on seven straight hours of sleep.

Today, according to the Pew Research Center, most pregnant women in the United States—82 percent—continue to work up until one month before giving birth. That's

a dramatic increase from fifty years ago, when only 44 percent of U.S. women worked at all during pregnancy. Even
so, morning sickness and exhaustion can make it hard to
keep up with meetings, travel, and deadlines. Giving birth
itself (which I've heard is as demanding as writing a book)
is the most physically painful experience many women
face. Then vaginal soreness, cramps, breast engorgement,
lower-belly pain after a C-section, hemorrhoids, and swell-
ing all make it unthinkable for many women to return to
work for several weeks after giving birth. Postpartum depression and lack of sleep can create an emotional maelstrom. And while breast-feeding is a beautiful thing, it also
can create logistical challenges, such as: *If I am at the office
for eight hours, how will my four-month-old eat?*

And the physical bond between a mother and her baby
embodies the mysterious and profound relational bond that
most women with children attest to. Perhaps because I have
never had children, or because I'm allergic to most things
sentimental, I didn't think much about the force of this bond
for years. Then, when I was twenty-eight, I went through a
personal crisis that kicked up some difficult dynamics between my parents and me. In that time, my mom and I got
into a fight, the kind that leaves you shaken and exhausted. I
said things to her that now embarrass me. Bewildered, she
responded through tears, "There is something that happens
when you have a child that can never be taken away, Kate.
You can't understand the kind of love that you have for your
own child, and I'm sorry that you might not experience it,
but that kind of bond never goes away."

My mom is not the sentimental type; I asked her recently if she misses having small kids at home, and without missing a beat, she said no. But in that moment of being at odds with one another, there resurfaced a deep and powerful bond between us—something about my bearing her likeness and yet being totally different; about all the care she poured into me, about how utterly dependent I was on her care, even on her body; about my instinct in times of crisis to call her before calling anyone else.

I recall this story not to build upon it a rule for what women with young kids should do, as if the powerful mother/child bond means all mothers must opt out of the workforce to stay home with their kids. Undoubtedly, the privileged West attaches to motherhood layers of cultural meaning that risk idealizing or sugarcoating it; as we reviewed in Chapter 4, mothers the world over cannot *not* work, because they must feed and clothe their children before emotionally bonding with them. Even still, the bond is one reason why many women find it hard to reenter the workforce after the slow marathon that is childbirth and early parenting.

Bosses

Before we blame everything on biology, we should also take a look at workplace policy. When it comes to the policies affecting the likelihood that women will return to work after giving birth, the United States looks retrograde—and even anti-family.

First, some statistics. According to the most recent numbers from the U.S. Department of Labor, 12 percent of

U.S. employees in the private sector are guaranteed access to paid family leave, either through generous employers or through public funds in five states. The U.S. Family and Medical Act of 1993 assures female employees twelve weeks of protected leave after pregnancy. This means— thank goodness—that a woman can't get fired for having a baby. But the protected leave isn't guaranteed paid, and the protection applies only to companies with at least fifty employees. Of the 170 developed countries with maternity benefit information, there are currently two that don't mandate financial assistance to women during maternity leave: the United States and Papua New Guinea.

Now, the situation in the United States *has* improved in the past half century, as more women having children have stayed in the workforce, thereby normalizing the totally reasonable desire not to be penalized at work for having a family. Before 1978, when Congress passed the Pregnancy Discrimination Act, it was legal for any company to fire a woman "on the basis of pregnancy, childbirth, or related medical conditions." Still, a tax "marriage penalty" for working wives, steeper child care costs, and a stall in wage adjustments for low-skilled workers (who are disproportionately women) keep many women from returning to work after having a baby.

Policy isn't just politics. Policy is always *personal,* shaping the lives of flesh-and-blood persons and their families. Take the story of Andrea Palpant Dilley, whom we met in Chapter 3. Andrea worked as a documentary producer for nine years at a small film company in Spokane, Washington. At work, "ninety percent of the people I worked with were male. They didn't have a leave policy of any kind," she told a room of women. Upon hearing this, many of us gasped. Dilley went on:

> Their company had been in existence for twenty-
> five years, and I was, to my knowledge, the first
> woman to get pregnant on the job. They didn't know
> anything about the Family and Medical Leave Act,
> which, incidentally, didn't apply because they were
> barely under the minimum employee requirement.
> I was left alone to go, "Here's what's normative out
> there"—maybe I could make some comparative
> arguments with comparably sized companies with
> women in comparable positions, so I had to do all
> this work while I was pregnant.

Andrea's efforts to advocate for herself didn't lead any-where—partly because there was no structural support in place at the company; and partly because her first child wouldn't take a bottle, to return to the biology barrier.

It was unsustainable, she says: "I was working twelve-hour days and getting paid for half of them." But Andrea also couldn't return to the company because, there was no *imaginative* space for women with established careers who got pregnant. "It came to this issue of integration," Andrea says. "You're a woman, and you had this one identity, and we knew what to do with you. And now you're pregnant."

"The workforce is created for men's lives," notes Ander-son. "Pensions, the way we structure everything, is faithful-ness to the company . . . you have men retiring from companies [after] thirty or forty years with the same company. How many women can actually do that?" Granted, this description was probably truer two generations ago; today's average U.S. employee switches jobs every 4.4 years. However, America's lagging paid maternity leave and anecdotes like Andrea's underscore the *gendered* notions of work we contend with, as well as the cultural inertia that leaves women like Andrea little choice but to leave work for a long period of time.

Official Bureau of Lady Judgment

The third barrier women face in seeking both career and family is, sadly, other women. Every group I met with for this book confirmed that we have not reached a cease-fire in the Mommy Wars, which rage not simply between women but also *within,* with constant guilt or second-guessing over the choices they are making about their families' lives.

One of the first shots in the so-called wars was Betty Friedan's 1963 *The Feminine Mystique,* considered by many the launch of feminism's second wave. Friedan, a journalist and a mother, documented the growing numbers of women after World War II whose role centered on being homemaker and mother. Despite the fact that advertisers and universities pitched the "housewife mother" as the fulfillment of the American Dream, women told Friedan that they felt lost, depressed, and surprised by their own ennui. "A woman today has been made to feel freakish and alone and guilty if she wants to be more than a husband's wife and children's mother, if she really wants to use her abilities in society," said Friedan.

To address "the problem that has no name," Friedan called women to join men in the offices and halls of public power. Granted, many women of her time—those of the lower and labor classes—were already working. Hence the most common critique of Friedan—one that's also made of Sandberg, Slaughter, and the like: The problem that has no name is mainly a privileged women's problem. However, Friedan and feminism's second wave brought some positive changes: equal pay, gender-neutral classified ads, maternity leave, and child care centers.

Unfortunately, the second wave of feminism also pitted women against each other, subtly denigrating home management and child-rearing. In the words of conservative commentator Carolyn Graglia, Friedan's feminism "was the attack on our intellectual capacity, that if we had a brain in our head, we couldn't be happy changing that baby's diaper." Many Christian leaders since Freidan's time have doubled down on the virtues of motherhood and homemaking, defending both against a perceived attack of "all traditional Judeo-Christian values." In the words of James Dobson, founder of the ministry Focus on the Family, "Everything understood to identify womanhood for thousands of years has been held up to ridicule and disdain. In a single decade, for example, the term 'housewife' became a symbol of exploitation, oppression, and . . . pardon the insult . . . stupidity. How strange!"

Actually, none of the women I interviewed for the book experienced direct ridicule and disdain. They were more likely to experience the Mommy Wars as a passive-aggressive skirmish, in statements like these:

- *I just don't know how you do it. It would be so hard for me to be away from my kids.*

- *I just don't know how you do it. I would get so bored at home.*

- *I just knew that I couldn't miss a day of my kids' lives.*

- *I just knew that, as an intelligent woman, I would be so unhappy spending all that time at home.*

Adding fuel to the Mommy Wars are many competing opinions about what a good mother looks like. When I was born, my parents had essentially one opinion, from Dr. Benjamin Spock, whose book *Baby and Child Care* sold fifty million copies and earned him the title "world's pediatrician." Today, scads of self-taught Spocks—in the form of mommy bloggers and social-media personalities—espouse what's best for all children everywhere, often with intense moralism around philosophies of child-rearing and consumer choices. Breast-feeding, attachment parenting, homemade versus store-bought food, homeschooling versus private versus public versus classical education, disciplinary strategies, sleep habits, potty training, and varying levels of gluten are all arenas in which mothers face overwhelming choices and overwhelming opinions. It's no wonder many mothers are a bit unsure that they are making the right decisions—and a bit defensive when someone suggests they are not.

Megan Slaboda has witnessed the Mommy Wars firsthand. A clothing designer, seamstress, and mother based in

Philadelphia, Slaboda knew she wanted to stay home with her kids for the first five years. During that time, she said, her social circles consisted of "very insecure women who weren't sure what they were supposed to do. They were having a kid, and they didn't know if they wanted to go back to work or stay home. . . . It was very hard, actually, to watch." Megan's line of work is more flexible than others—"you can't take a sewing machine everywhere, but people can come to you." And her husband, a pastor, spent time at home while earning his Ph.D. But as her kids grow up, "I'm having a very hard time getting back in my work world," says Megan. "There are so many different conversations in my head, listening to everybody."

Less Balance, More Integration

If you have read up to this point hoping that I will offer foolproof breakthroughs for these barriers, the rest of this chapter will be a letdown. No one can offer a one-size-fits-all solution to ensure that all women *can* have it all, all the time. I can't balance my own single-lady life, let alone yours.

But as we contend with biology, bosses, and boards of lady judgment, there are many small things we can do to lighten one another's load, to help us all pursue good professional work and good parenting work at the same time.

We can start by ditching the phrase "work/life balance," for the way it pits work and home against each other, as if they are opposing forces to be constantly tamed and managed. As if they are foes instead of crucial partners in a

flourishing life lived before God. Instead, we need to begin talking about work/home *integration*—and seeing our spouses and churches and friends as players in the pursuit of that full human life.

That means we can start thinking about work and home belonging to the family, with each family able to discern whose gifts and dispositions are best expressed in each sphere. That means the work/life integration is a conversation for both women and men. Many wives will discern that they are best suited to being at home with little kids in the first few years, while many husbands will discern that they are best suited to earn income outside the home in those years. But this setup will be helpful so long as it stays *descriptive*—describing unique flesh-and-blood people with distinct gifts. It will be destructive if it is offered primarily as *prescriptive*—fitting men and women into roles that are afield of their actual God-given gifts and desires.

Another small thing we can do—especially in church discipleship—is to help husbands grasp the broad historical Christian vision for marriage and fatherhood. "The family is the most basic of all vocations, the one in which God's creative power and His providential care are most dramatically conveyed through human beings," notes theologian and educator Gene Edward Veith, Jr. Drawing on Martin Luther—who wrote widely on the dignity of all "ordinary" work—Veith says the call to marriage and family is not ultimately about authority, as in "Who has to obey whom?" Rather, he writes, "the Scriptures and the doctrine of vocation teach that the purpose of every vocation is to love and serve your neighbor." A husband's closest neighbor is his wife and children, and he has an enormous chance to bless them in shared daily life.

To a person, every woman I met who worked outside the home while raising young children said that she could do neither well without her husband's *full support of her calling*. This is what Catherine Crouch, a physicist and educator at Swarthmore College outside Philadelphia, identifies as the primary backbone for her academic work (a career path that can be quite inflexible for women with children). In Catherine's words—spoken, fittingly, while her husband, Andy, was preparing dinner in the background—"You cannot underestimate the importance of having your spouse believe in what you are doing as you go through the years of trying to combine childrearing and professional work." She continues:

> A common challenge faced by Christian women trying to both raise a family and work outside the home is that it is relatively rare to feel that the community as a whole supports you, so if your spouse doesn't support you, you are really dead in the water. . . . The fact that the Christian community looks at least bemusedly if not askance [laughs] at women trying to do what I'm doing, that makes it more of a challenge for spouses to be supportive. The most critical thing is the agreement by both spouses that both of you are doing what you are called to do. Then exactly how you manage the kind of nitty-gritty of the kind of labor can vary a lot.

In the classic book *The Family: A Christian Perspective on the Contemporary Home,* family therapists and scholars Jack and Judith Balswick say a biblical marriage is one in which "both the mother and the father are actively involved in the parenting process." It has "flexible and interchangeable roles as each occasion calls forth what is needed." They note that Scripture doesn't treat the mother as more important for a child's well-being than the father. In fact, the Bible speaks much more of fathers than of mothers, calling men to lead and love as *patriarchs* (lit. "family ruling") in their homes. The Balswicks note—and sociological studies confirm—that "the lack of effective fathering often relates to breakdown in the family system." Thus, women's staying power in the workplace presents a chance for more men to invest in fatherhood, to find a fulfillment in leading and loving their children that many fathers of the past two generations barely knew.

"For Americans of every social class, the future of marriage will be more egalitarian, with more shared burdens and blurrier divisions of labor, or it will not be at all," notes *New York Times* columnist Ross Douthat. Indeed, a majority of American men and women now identify "egalitarian marriages"—in which both partners work, do housework, and take care of the children—as more satisfying than traditional marriages, in which the husband works to provide for the family and the wife takes care of the house and children.[30] Tasks and roles long considered fixed in biology or

---

30. Rampell, Catherine. "What Men (and Women) Want in a Marriage Today vs. yesterday," *The Washington Post,* December 12, 2014, http://www.washingtonpost.com/news/rampage/wp/2014/12/09/what-men-and-women-want-in-a-marriage-today-vs-yesterday/.

spiritual design are being traded, shared, and handed off at increasing rates.

The new marriage model can be messy. In the traditional model, at least, everyone knows his or her job. With sharing of responsibilities comes more late-night conversations hashing out who's taking care of what, when trade-offs will happen, who will enter and exit the workforce and when. Despite its messiness, the new marriage model is also an invitation: for husbands and wives to pursue a family vocation—to craft a culture of industry, interdependency, and love, all for their children to thrive.

A Dad Is Not a Babysitter

But to make work/family integration a family issue, we will need to stop praising men for doing the plain work of parenting.

This means Christian communities can raise the bar for fathers. This is a regular topic of conversation for Tish Harrison Warren and her husband, Jonathan, both ordained Anglican priests. "The expectation for fathers in our culture is so low, as long as I don't cheat on you, beat anyone, [and] talk to my children, tell them I love them sometimes, I am the dad of the year," notes Jonathan. "But the expectations on moms are to be awesome moms and do everything else." One example: Look for a woman buying groceries with children in tow. They are ubiquitous, so we barely notice them. But a man buying groceries with children in tow will be cooed over: "What a good dad! What a lucky wife you have!"

Our generally low expectation for fathers is one reason that many men can have it all without even realizing it. Peter Chin is a pastor, writer, and father of five children based in Washington, D.C. He notes that a low "level of participation in a child's life still allows a man enough time and energy to fully devote themselves to another calling, that of their professional lives. . . . *This* is why men are better able to balance these two roles—not because of the enhanced abilities of men, but because the role of father is culturally diminished and relatively lightweight."

Yet what if the men who seem to have it all actually don't? What if they are missing out on a beautiful, challenging core part of their development, on a part of life where they learn to be gentle, nurturing, even soft? Where they don't have to fight for their place in the pecking order, as so many men do at work? Implicit in the conversation is an invitation to men to reinvest in the vocation of family—to work with their hands at mundane tasks, to take joy in their children, and to find meaning and identity outside a paycheck and colleagues' praise.

However the particular tasks get doled out in the new marriage model, there's the bedrock truth that two are better than one, that God means for marriages to spill over into shalom far beyond the nuclear family, that a marriage can be a catalyst for pursuing our work with excellence and care. Dorcas Cheng-Tozun, based in San Francisco, worked in the nonprofit sector for ten years, traveling regularly and finding fulfillment in the work. Simultaneously, she experienced major burnout and had a baby. Today, she is a writer, and her husband leads a nonprofit that serves many in the developing world. While these days her husband has the more visible, high-powered job, the couple understands that their roles could switch at any time. "There's this picture that God brings together of how you are going to serve and work in the world, and everybody plays some part in that," said Cheng-Tozun.

A Pro-Family Agenda

It's never a direct line from scriptural principle to public policy. But Christians of all political stripes can agree that highly skilled, faithful employees should not be penalized for making the beautiful choice to have a child. In fact, paid family leave for mothers (and fathers!) could be one of the most unifying pro-family policies championed by Christians.

At the time of this writing, Daniel Murphy had secured his status as a home-run superstar, batting .421 for the New York Mets in the 2015 post-season and clinching the team's fifth National League pennant (to this casual Cubs fan's sadness). The year prior, Murphy, an evangelical Christian, had ruffled sports commentators' feathers by taking a three-day leave of absence in order to be present at his son's birth. Here is how he explained that decision at the White House's 2014 Working Families Summit:

> When [my son] Noah asks me one day, "What happened? What was it like when I was born?" I could have answered, "Well, Stephen Strasburg hung me a breaking ball that day, son. I slammed it into the right field corner." . . . But I'm the one who cut his

umbilical cord. And long after they've told me I'm not good enough to play baseball anymore, I'll be a father and a husband.

The reason Murphy chose to be there for his son's birth? "We try to take Jesus Christ and we try to put him in the center of everything."

Murphy attended his son's birth because he knew that welcoming a new life is more important than career success. Many U.S. workers—Christian and otherwise, middle-class and working-class, men and women—share his conviction. They should be allowed to attend to a child's needs, especially in those precious first months, without being penalized at work. More companies are realizing that paid family leave is good business practice; it helps retain strong employees, especially women who would have dropped out in previous decades. And happy workers produce better work.

In the coming election season, we can expect Democrat and Republican leaders to debate the merits of paid family leave and who should ensure it: namely, the federal government or privately owned businesses. Whatever the solution, Christians can agree that motherhood and fatherhood will be honored when the workplace honors the sacredness of new life—and puts money on the line to show it.

Buckets and Buckets of Grace

Grace is a good place to end a chapter on motherhood. Perhaps more than anything, what today's moms need is grace. Grace to endure the evolving nap schedules and temper tantrums and moralistic mommy blogs and sheer exhaustion. Grace to make the right decisions for a child, even when those decisions are different from a peer's. Grace to know that God sees and delights in a mother's love for her children, in all the ways that love could be expressed.

During a group discussion in San Francisco, writer Bronwyn Lea confessed that her first year of motherhood was "brutal to [my] sense of identity." Because it was her primary task that year, she approached it like she would any job: researching meticulously to find the "best" way of doing motherhood. When other parents confidently proclaim that another way is the best way, "it feels like an attack," she said. It took "buckets and buckets of grace" from friends at church for Bronwyn to come to peace with her parenting decisions. "Anybody who is trying to attach their identity to performance as a parent is setting themselves up for tons of tears. There are no gold stars."

I'm nowhere close to being a mom, but I have seen the way motherhood is set up to be a performance among people who should know the most about grace. How motherhood can become a dividing line between supposedly righteous and unrighteous women in a community. Young mothers I know have been reduced to tears because older mothers at church felt it was their duty to "strongly recommend" attachment parenting. That philosophy encourages as much physical and emotional contact as possible in a baby's first years, entailing breast-feeding, co-sleeping, and often cloth diapering and homemade baby food. It's like the extreme sport of motherhood. Obviously, these moms praised attachment parenting because they found a lot of good in it. But not every mom will or can or should. And on matters about which Scripture is silent, it is best to extend to each other freedom rather than create new rules for holiness.

Throughout my research, I heard time and again that when women had a pursuit outside children, they felt they were better moms. When they could spend even a few hours a week doing something they loved, they felt more attentive to their children. When they could use their gifts and education outside the home, they felt like they could model meaningful work for their children, especially their daughters. When they could invest in their own development as persons, they found they had more of a person to offer their children. "There are so many ways that we provide for and form our children," said Laura Waters Hinson. "A big part of that is the parents themselves: Who are they becoming and what kind of person are they modeling for their child? It's not just limited to, 'Did I stay home with my child from ages one through five?'"

Whatever you do decide for your family, reader, may you know in a tangible, embodied way that there are buckets and buckets of grace for you.

Amy Orr-Ewing

$\mathcal{A}$s director of the Oxford Centre for Christian Apologetics (OCCA), Amy Orr-Ewing is one of today's most prominent UK apologists. Ironically, she learned to communicate the gospel in a place where she wasn't allowed to speak at all.

It was 1996, and Orr-Ewing and two friends felt called to travel to Afghanistan to try to meet with Taliban leaders. They had the editor of an Oxford student newspaper issue a letter explaining that they were journalists, one of the few groups permitted into the country at the time. Upon arrival in Herat, the students were transported to a hidden apartment, passed several checkpoints without a hitch, and, quite improbably, invited to one of the Taliban's secret military headquarters. There, Amy wasn't allowed to speak and almost wasn't allowed in.

The students were escorted into a room filled with guards holding Kalashnikov rifles. Over several hours, the two male students asked several questions, like good journalists. As they were about to leave, one of them handed a Taliban leader a Pashto translation of the Bible. His eyes widened. "I know exactly what this book is," he said. "I've been praying to God for years that I could read the Bible. I'll read it every day until I finish it."

Amy shared this story with me while I was visit-

ing OCCA's headquarters in 2014, on assignment for *Christianity Today* magazine. It's a story she has shared many times in apologetics talks and in the book *Holy Warriors,* cowritten with her fellow traveler to Afghanistan and now husband, Francis "Frog." "We discovered that at the heart of the world's most fundamentalist Islamic regime, there was someone praying that God would send him a Bible, and God chose us to do that," Amy told me. "Gospel proclamation can happen in impossible places."

Today, Amy is proclaiming the gospel in another impossible place. Granted, you won't find Oxford dons leading tutorials with Kalashnikovs in hand. But you will find cynicism and an existential shrug toward the faith still reflected in Oxford's motto: *Dominus illuminatio mea*—"the Lord is my light." While UK church attendance is faltering, vestiges of Christian faith still mark the psychosocial landscape in Britain. The work of the apologist is to bring Christianity to bear on the challenges of human life, not simply to run it through a clinical test of verifiability.

This is where apologists like Amy may have an edge on their male counterparts.

"Amy has good relational skills, which is important," says Alister McGrath, noted apologist and founder of OCCA. "She's not a lecturer delivering a talk in a disengaged way. Apologetics is reaching out from the churches to our culture. We need the range of speakers and experiences to connect up with that culture."

Sharon Dirckx, who earned a Ph.D. in brain imaging before becoming an OCCA tutor, agrees. "Amy has an amazing capacity to think rationally through a problem and present it coherently—but with compassion," she says. "Amy has the heart of a mother and the mind of a theologian. The combination is powerful."

Amy began preaching as a teenager in her father's church; in 1998, she became the first woman to join the itinerant preaching team of Ravi Zacharias International Ministries. She went on to earn a first-class degree (given to a fraction of Oxford students) in theology at Christ Church before earning a master's in theology at King's College London. Now—amid OCCA lectures, talks throughout the UK, the States, and Southeast Asia, and raising three boys with Frog—she is also completing a Ph.D. at Oxford on the apologetics work of Dorothy Sayers.

Frog is a ministry powerhouse in his own right, having been the youngest incumbent in the Church of England. Today, he pastors a young congregation that meets on a farm in Buckinghamshire, a wealthy suburb halfway between Oxford and London. As he told me, "Amy and I don't believe there's a tension between these two jobs. There are many timetable crashes, but it's a diarizing, juggling match rather than a calling thing. I've always tried to invest in apologetics ministry, and Amy is utterly committed to the local church.

"Since Amy started young, there weren't that many

role models she could spot, where the woman is the preacher who travels and the guy is the one who stays local. Now that's becoming much more normal. A couple where both work—there's going to have to be give and take."

When she started with RZIM, Amy was the only woman on the speaking circuit. Today, ten of RZIM's thirty-six itinerant speakers are women. OCCA graduate Alycia Wood says Amy has been the role model that Amy herself lacked. "Women face unique challenges as apologists because of the demands of travel, and that many events are in the evenings or on the weekends. I learned a lot by watching Amy be a brilliant apologist and an excellent mother to three boys." That Orr-Ewing does both informs the Zacharias Trust's flexible workplace culture, one that doesn't force female staff to opt out of teaching and traveling should they choose to have a family.

"We need men and women ready to make disciples of all nations," says Dirckx. "If you let women use their gifts as evangelists, you have the potential for reaching more people. In the West, it's a numbers game, isn't it?"

And what may seem like a practical concession is really a bedrock truth of Christianity: God has always used unlikely people—like three Oxford students pretending to be journalists—to resound the Good News. "Without women, we wouldn't know what happened at

the Cross," says Amy. "John's there, but all the other witnesses to the words from the cross are female. And women are the first witnesses to the Resurrection.

"If you're a Christian, you believe the Lord arranged for that. That's not unintentional. That's amazing."

CHAPTER SEVEN

A Fruitful Life

In the book-lined living room of my friend Shelly[31] and her husband hangs a print of a painting that has long captivated my imagination. Printed in fine black ink on thin cloth is Shelly's family tree, rendered as a literal tree. Every descendant is remembered in branches and shoots, an intricate genealogy that reaches to the heavens.

Dating back to 1746, Shelly's family tree includes six generations of more than 1,300 individuals. It reflects an era in which the family—past and present—was the center of life and identity. Children lived close to their parents, even when they were grown and had children of their own. A grandmother would move in with her son and daughter-in-law, bringing mirth and perhaps a bit of terror from the west wing of the farmhouse. Children would learn from an aunt or uncle or cousin how to shoot a duck or sew a quilt or bring in the cows at day's end. During those times, I imagine, it was easier than it is now to remember this central truth: No one can exist apart from others, uniting and

---

31. Name has been changed to protect identity.

bearing life and adding his or her own line of ink to the story of humanity.

The first time I saw Shelly's family tree, I was twenty-four. I was growing aware that I probably would add my own little branches to the great tree of life. But the thought was abstract. Though I had dated men, none of them had inspired thoughts of marriage, let alone children. The painting fascinated me in a detached way. How intricate and folksy, something you might buy at Anthropologie (for the price of a car).

The second time I saw Shelly's family tree, I was twenty-nine. A friend and I were visiting her and her husband for a weekend of apple picking and whiskey sipping (when in Kentucky). In the five years since I first saw the family tree, many of my friends had nestled into married life and begun having children. Invitations to baby showers and baptisms had started trickling in. Seeing articles about pregnancy complications for women over a certain age now brought me a twinge of worry. And I had dated at least one person who'd inspired thoughts of marriage, and babies, and baby names.

And on this trip, I noticed a detail in the family tree that I hadn't seen before: On many of the branches were offshoots that didn't go anywhere. Esther was born in 1787 and died in 1826, and Anne was born in 1856 and died in 1923, and William was born in 1872 and died in 1905. These people, created and loved and known intimately by God, never added new branches to the tree of life. They were depicted as stumps. And these stumps made me very sad.

I also wondered about the particular turns and contours of Esther's and Anne's and William's lives. Was William the eccentric uncle known for his tall tales and roaring laugh? Did Anne ever have a suitor sit down with her parents to a marriage proposal? Did they make things or create things—a recipe, a bench, a quilt, a new method of tapping trees or fixing fences—that are now forgotten to history? Most important, did they know themselves to be part of a bigger family tree, one whose branches are constituted by the grooves in the hard wood of a cross?

Finding a Seat at the Table of Womanhood

In researching this book, I met many single women who are spending this season of their lives centered on work. Some of them want very much to be married, and they experience pain around that. Some of them are fully enjoying the single life and don't think that much about marriage. Some of them are open to marriage if the right person comes along.

All of the women are united in this: They need a vision of a fruitful Christian life that incorporates more than marriage. Professional women who are single, who spend a majority of their time pouring themselves into their work, show us that there is more than one way to live a fruitful life as a Christian. But in order for these women to bear such fruit, they will need a spiritual framework, as well as practical support, that encourages and equips them to be professionally fruitful.

As we develop a positive theology of work for women, the word that best captures their work in this season, and perhaps for life, is "fruitfulness." Fruitfulness is simply all the ways that our God-given resources—time and energy and bodies and brains and relationships—are invested in order to bear seeds of shalom in and for God's world.

Fruitfulness is closely related to the word "steward-ship," in that it gives us language to account for what we do with what we have been given. It's more than "industry" or even "work," since fruitfulness encompasses all the dimensions of life, from paid to unpaid work, from the office to the home and everywhere in between. But for many single women, paid work is where they invest most of themselves and bear the most kingdom fruit. That is true for me in this season and perhaps for life.

A mother and father are tasked with the centrally important work of stewarding a child's life, raising her in love, correction, and understanding of God. Children are a concrete image of the Genesis 1 command to "be fruitful and multiply." However, if we trace the full arc of Scripture, we learn that fruitfulness extends far beyond having children. Single or married, children or none, each of us is accountable for taking whatever God has given us—say, a college degree, a pay raise, a supportive community, a scholarship, a trip to another country or culture—and putting it all to good use, for the benefit of others and as a signpost of God's redemptive work in the world.

In the previous chapter, we met women who are stewarding the calls to work and to raise children simultaneously. To write the chapter, I depended on other women telling me what this looks like on the ground. But I write this chapter as someone in her early thirties who has grappled deeply with what it might mean to be fruitful as a single person.

I say "grappling" more often than "joyfully living out in freedom" for a couple of reasons. The first is that I desire to be married, and I imagine that, should I meet a man with whom I could build a life, children would be desired, though not guaranteed (as they aren't for anyone). My singleness has arisen from circumstance, not choice.

The second is that I live in the suburbs of Chicago, close to Wheaton College, a leading Christian university. The area is as much a magnet for educated, earnest, evangelical Christians for whom marriage and family seem the natural way of things, as it is a genuinely pleasant place to live. Here, bearing and raising children are primary ways that my peers live into the call to fruitfulness, and that's all to the good. But in the steady stream of strollers and Ergo carriers and discussions about breast-feeding and making organic baby food and whether the hue of a diaper's contents is normal, I have wondered if there's a place for me at the table of womanhood and fruitfulness alike; I have wondered whether we Christians place our hope in a tree bigger than the family heirlooms that hang on our walls.

The truth is that, outside Wheaton, Illinois, my tribe is growing. The number of unmarried adults in the United States continues to increase year by year, with nearly half (44 percent) of Americans over age eighteen now single. Of all single Americans, 62 percent have never been married. Christian women in particular face the perennial dearth of single Christian men: Among eighteen-to-twenty-nine-year-old church attendees today, 57 percent are women and 43 percent are men. According to the Austin Institute, these numbers run parallel with female/male ratios on today's four-year college campuses.

All of this means that U.S. churches can expect more single women to show up at their doors in the years to come. As more Christian women graduate from college and dive not directly into marriage but into full-time professions, investing themselves there for years or decades, they will need a broader Christian community that knows what to do with them.

The Single/Married Church Divide

It is patently true that single professional women are a subgroup within a subgroup of many churches. Their professional work alienates them from churches that treat full-time ministry as "best." And their singleness alienates them from churches where marriage and children are normative. As I spoke with many bright, grounded, inspiring, and beautiful Christian women whose energies and passions are poured into professional work, I heard a recurring theme of isolation.

Before she became a children's book author and creative writing instructor, Jennifer Trafton Peterson was the managing editor of *Christian History* magazine (a onetime sister publication of my employer). With a master's in church history and religious studies from Duke University, Jennifer led the beloved magazine as it covered everything from J. S. Bach to Gnosticism to George MacDonald's influence on C. S. Lewis. But while she edited some of the

top historians of the church, Jennifer describes this period
as "a very dark time, very lonely":

> I hopped from church to church for four years,
> never able to settle into one community, because
> I found myself falling in the cracks between the
> typical categories of urban middle-class churchgo-
> ers: the younger college and grad school students,
> the families, the older divorcees, etc. As a thirty-
> ish never-married professional woman, I felt as if
> churches didn't know what to do with me.
>
> I would look at the programs and small group
> offerings, and there just seemed to be an assump-
> tion that if I was past college age and female, then
> I either needed a MOPS [Mothers of Preschoolers]
> group or a Beth Moore Bible study. Most of the
> women my age were moms, and I felt a social bar-
> rier there that I didn't know how to cross. My job
> and my interests often gave me more in common
> with men, but I wanted to be so careful never to
> look as if I were ignoring their wives.

So while her work united her with men who were also
focused on their careers, she felt uncomfortable spending
too much time with them. Now married and living in Nashville, Jennifer says that marriage hasn't fully erased the oth-
erness she feels as a woman without children.

Andrea Lucado, a writer and publicist, also based in
Nashville, helps lead a group for teen girls at her church.
She notices that the other leader, who is also twenty-eight
but is married with children, fields most of the girls' ques-

tions. "Their desires are to get married and have kids, and I wonder if they see me as an adult," says Lucado. "They have never asked me about my work, though they have asked me plenty about dating and marriage." While we can't blame teen girls for being excited about dating and boys, these girls, it seems, hadn't been prompted to think about what they would do with their skills, passions, and education once leaving high school.

Christena Cleveland, professor of the practice of reconciliation at Duke Divinity School, has drawn attention in the past few years to the racial divisions that continue to plague many American churches. Yet in a 2013 blog post that generated 330 comments, Cleveland addressed another deep divide in the church: the one between married and single people.

Noting that the vast majority of people "calling the shots" in churches and ministries are married, Cleveland wrote that single people are often "misunderstood, ignored, overlooked for leadership positions, caricatured, equated with immaturity, and little more than a punchline or an afterthought." As a regular conference speaker, Cleveland says, she is most frequently asked: "How come you're not married?" In a list of six steps that married Christians can take to embrace single adults, she writes:

> We might not be walking down the aisle or gestating a baby, but God is doing some amazing things in our lives—from the "monumental" (such as helping us obtain degrees, launch ministries/businesses, pay off college loans) to the "mundane"

(such as helping us serve our neighborhoods, pray
for each other).

I can honestly say I have never felt that my marital status impeded my work as managing editor of *Christianity
Today*. While marriage and parenting play a crucial role in
many people's sanctification, neither is apparently needed
for being a decent editor and leader. I'm also grateful that I
spent my twenties at a small Anglican/Episcopal church
where other churchgoers regularly asked me about my
nine-to-five job and had me speak about my work in more
than one adult education class.

At the same time, the Anglican tradition has rituals and
set-aside times for honoring marriage and children in a way
that it just doesn't for professional work and vocation. The
Book of Common Prayer includes gorgeous liturgies to accompany marriage and baptism. It includes prayers for "vocation in daily work" that ask God to bless all who labor.
That said, there is no liturgy set aside to bless and honor
those who, say, are beginning a faculty post or a medical ro-
tation, or starting a nonprofit, or retiring after fifty years of
teaching.

The gap in the liturgy is less painful than the social gap
I have occasionally experienced in church. Compared with
that of many friends and peers, my time in local churches
has been relatively painless. Often the pain has had more to
do with my own "ouchie" places than the intent of others.
But sometimes simple blindness can lead to as much pain
as malice.

I will never forget standing in a group of five women

after Sunday-morning worship in summer 2014. Of the five, three were pregnant, and together they had six children (already). I was literally, awkwardly, seated so that I was staring at three pregnant bellies encircling me. There was no way to enter the conversation, because it was about the particularities of pregnancy, and none of the women tried to let me in. A couple of the women were commiserating that getting pregnant again soon would throw a wrench in their families' plans and finances. "Please, God, don't send us another baby right now!" one said. It was like exclaiming, "Please, God, you're blessing us *too* much! We just can't take any more blessings!" Standing in that group of women—all lovely individuals, by the way—I felt more invisible and alone than I do around male colleagues my dad's age.

Stories like these from individual women don't mean that churches should stop honoring and teaching on marriage and parenting, calls that are blessed and honored by Scripture and the Christian tradition. It doesn't mean that they need to cancel the Father's Day cookout or the MOPS Bible study. It does mean, practically speaking, that churches where the common life centers on the family will have a harder time attracting and incorporating women (and men) who invest primarily in their work rather than in a spouse or children, for a season or for life. As more American women stay unmarried or childless for long stretches of time, churches will need to find ways to speak to and honor other forms of gospel fruitfulness.

The same is true for leaders at Christian college campuses—environments expressly intended to prepare students for vocational fruitfulness after graduation.

The Mrs. Degree Won't Go Away

To research this book, I met with a small group of juniors and seniors at Wheaton College, a top evangelical university just minutes from where I live and work. I also met with a dozen or so young women enrolled in the Scholar's Semester, a study-abroad program in Oxford, England, affiliated with the Council for Christian Colleges and Universities. Women in both groups, I learned, were experiencing mixed messages as they looked ahead to life after graduation.

On the one hand, the women indicated that their professors were preparing them to become "world changers" and "agents of renewal"—two popular Christian college slogans—in whatever field they were entering. Among these women, that included international law, public policy, international medicine, theater, and ancient history.

While she found that some of her male classmates weren't especially supportive, "the male professors really invest in us," says Elle Ryan (now Crawford), a philosophy major at Shorter University in Rome, Georgia. "One very strong female professor in the department does as well. She calls out the female students and helps us to formulate our own vision of what we could do after college." At Gordon College, English major Christy Urbano says, an annual panel discussion open to students highlights multiple life choices made by female faculty. The panel features "a woman who stayed home and raised her kids, someone who worked part-time [while raising kids], and one of my professors who is single," says Christy. "For women, there's a cost no matter what path you choose. They try to open the conversation and see what the challenges are in each sphere." Further, all of the students I spoke with said that vocation and calling were regular topics of conversation—sometimes to a fault—on their campuses.

On the other hand, many of the young women indicated that a marriage-obsessed subculture persisted on campus, and that pressure was hard to square with the world-changer aspirations set before them. Peers, parents, and official events like floor dates and football banquets at times obscured the primary reason they were enrolled in college. Emily Lund, an English major at George Fox University in Newberg, Oregon, remembers friends and folks from church joking about her getting her MRS. degree:

> No one talked about men going to get their MR. degrees. There's no equivalent for that . . . there's still that undercurrent of: Women can go to college, but while they're there, you might meet someone, and that will change the course of your life. I do know people at my school who are just waiting, hoping they'll find the one. That wasn't on my radar at all when I went, but in a way, it was because other people put it there.

Other students I spoke with struggled to find role models and mentors. Even though there are more women than men in her major, Joy Clarkson of Biola University

says, "I see a lot of my male peers . . . getting a mentor relationship. No matter how hard I try, there's a certain level
that I can't quite get that same mentorship relationship
because it feels socially awkward or could be viewed as in-
appropriate."

A couple of the Wheaton students expressed a similar
lack of support. They had been selected to attend Praxis
Academy, a four-day event for students from more than
thirty Christian colleges to train to become "a new generation of entrepreneurs to create impact and shape culture."
After the event during the summer of 2014, the male
Wheaton students went on an informal weekend retreat to
continue brainstorming and networking with male Wheaton alumni. The women I spoke with wondered if female
students should have been invited, and more generally
longed for more practical support for stepping into their
own careers.

Many young people do meet their spouses at college; I
think back on my own experience at Calvin College and realize that I probably won't ever be surrounded again by that
many Christian men concentrated in one place. In theory,
anyone can be a world changer and a wife and mother at
the same time. But at just the moment in their lives when
young Christian women are being prepared for and launching into professional fruitfulness, they are hearing a lot
about other kinds of fruitfulness. To be honest, it seems
like a wasted opportunity for Christian college educators.

All the Single Ladies

One helpful resource for these women—and for churches that want to practically support professional single women—is in the history of God's people. Of all the women who shine most brilliantly in the history of the church, a striking number never married or remained widows for most of their lives.

We see women in the early church bearing fruit for the gospel as it spread throughout Turkey, Greece, and Rome. Significantly, their partner in the gospel, Paul, had converted from a tradition in which men couldn't make eye contact with women who weren't family members, to a faith in which women were "fellow contenders for the gospel" (Phil. 4:1–3). Lydia, whom we met in Chapter 4, was a successful businesswoman and almost certainly a widow, and she opened her home to Paul and other early leaders in the church of Philippi. Phoebe, like Lydia, was a woman of means and either unmarried or widowed when she became "a benefactor of many" for Paul and ministers in the church of Cenchreae. And while her name is tossed to and fro in debates on women's spiritual leadership, early church fathers and many biblical scholars today agree that Iounias—Junia—was a woman "prominent among the apostles" (Rom. 16:7). Even if some of these women were married and widowed, their work for God, rather than their marital status or ability to have children, was what Paul commended.

In a time when religious life was almost uniformly patriarchal, unmarried women witnessed to the gospel, often in ways radically counter to Greco-Roman and traditional Jewish society alike. As Christine Colon and Bonnie Field note in *Singled Out: Why Celibacy Must Be Reinvented in Today's Church,* "The Roman government penalized the unmarried and the childless, and Judaism still maintained that the survival of Israel depended on marriage." As such, a woman's countercultural virginity "allowed them a powerful voice that asserted that they belonged to God."[32] For virgin martyrs such as the slave Blandina (d. 177) and Agnes (d. 303), gospel work was witnessing that Christ held the ultimate claim on their lives—and their deaths. Fabiola, from a family of means in fourth-century Rome, invested her wealth and energy after becoming a widow into founding a hospital. Similarly, Macrina, who swore off marriage after her fiancé died, informed the theology of her brothers, Gregory of Nyssa and Basil. She helped to establish a monastery and a hospital in Caesarea.

Monasteries of the Middle Ages became arenas where unmarried women bore fruit in the form of education, spiritual discipline, and care for the sick, poor, and dying. As academic Mary Skinner writes, such monasteries provided "education for girls[,] . . . second careers for widows and wives, and an alternative to marriage for young girls."[33] Some monastic leaders stand out for their theological contributions. After receiving permission to record her famed, ecstatic mystical visions, Hildegard of Bingen (1098–1179)

---

32. Page 179.

33. Skinner, Mary. "Benedictine Life for Women in Central France, 850–1100: A Feminist Revival," as quoted in Colon and Field, *Singled Out,* 182.

became the first women permitted by the pope to write a book of theology. At age nineteen, Catherine of Siena (1347–1380) had a vision of Christ placing a ring upon her finger to signal their spiritual union. Shortly after, Catherine dedicated herself to nursing neighbors struck by the Black Death of the late fourteenth century. She began writing and visiting political leaders to demand reform of the excesses of the state and the Catholic Church, portending the Protestant Reformation. She and two other single women— Teresa of Avila (1515–1582) and Thérèse of Lisieux (1873–1897)—are the only women named "Doctors of the Church" in the Catholic tradition.

While the Reformation charged the role of wife and mother with spiritual duty, the missionary zeal of the eighteenth and nineteenth centuries sent many single women into the international mission field—a radical choice in a time without international data plans and health insurance.

From an early age, Charlotte "Lottie" Digges Moon felt a strong call to international missions. Even though her Baptist community was reluctant to send an unmarried woman into the field, in 1873 she became the Southern Baptist Convention's first female missionary to China. Moon founded schools for women, spoke out against foot binding, and, during a famine, gave away her rations so that the people she served could survive. The annual Lottie Moon Christmas Offering for Missions has raised more than $1.5 billion since the Southern Baptist Convention established it in 1888.

Other single missionaries—Gertrude Howe, also in

China; Amy Carmichael in India; Maude Cary in North Africa; Johanna Veenstra in Nigeria; and Rachel Saint in Ecuador—gave the burgeoning missionary movement of the nineteenth and twentieth centuries much fortitude and zeal. I'll give Elisabeth Elliot—the queen mother of lady missionaries—the final word. Elliot, who lived as a widow after her husband, Jim, was killed in Ecuador in 1956, wrote:

> Your education or lack of it, your tastes and prejudices and fears and status or ambitions, your age or sex or color or height or marital status or income bracket are all things which may be offered to God, after you have presented your bodies as a living sacrifice. And God knows exactly what to do with them. They are not obstacles if you hand them over.

In fact, what feels like an obstacle often is the very foundation of our kingdom fruitfulness. On Valentine's Day 2013, Sarah Thebarge, a writer and speaker based in Portland, noted for *Sojourners* magazine that many heroines of church history were single women. She wrote, "[T]he women who were 'deprived' of marriage actually thrived and made a significant impact in the world—not *in spite* of their singleness but likely *because* of it."

Thebarge is an example of the fruit God draws from the lives of single women. At age twenty-seven, she was diagnosed with breast cancer, undergoing a bilateral mastectomy, chemotherapy, and radiation over eighteen months. During this time, her boyfriend of two years broke up with her, and she nearly died of sepsis.

Crushed, she moved to Portland to put the pieces of her life back together. On a train ride, she met a mother from Somalia and her five girls. Sarah learned that the Somali family had no clothes, no furniture, and few prospects of survival, with the mother scrounging moldy bread out of Dumpsters to feed her girls. In her beautiful book, *The Invisible Girls*, Thebarge tells of befriending the mother and her children. It turned attention away from her own pain and helped the girls thrive in America. Where there had been death and pain, God brought new life through Thebarge's ministry.

God has brought new life out of my pain, too.

New Provisions

For a long time, in my heart of hearts, I didn't believe I could bear fruit apart from marriage and children. Or, I assumed, whatever fruit I bore as a professional was not as lasting or important as the kind I would bear in a family. No one has a work tree hanging above the mantel.

If you read the Introduction, then you know that in 2012, I was engaged to a man with whom I envisioned living life together. At the time, I was an associate editor at *Christianity Today*. I deeply enjoyed the work, having cofounded the Her.meneutics women's site in 2009 and recently become editorial director of a project called This Is Our City. I got to travel across the country, interview fascinating people, and make some weighty editorial decisions. I planned to continue working remotely for the magazine after marriage.

With my engagement came a slow shift in how I thought about my professional life, which seemed like it would take a backseat in the car of Katelyn's identity. I began to feel that I had to choose to be either a successful worker and a halfhearted wife and mother; or a committed wife and mother and a halfhearted worker. And I wanted to be fully dedicated to both.

Likewise, I assumed that marriage would give me a new purpose and direction—that it would provide a clear answer to the question of identity. It would definitely secure me a place at the table of womanhood; in conversations about whether Bumbo seats are safe and how to establish a successful nap schedule, I would have something to say. I wanted to be married not only because I genuinely wanted to spend my life with the person I was engaged to but also because I wanted questions of identity and security tied up in a neat bow.

There was to be no neat bow. The engagement was messy; the ending, even messier. That's all I can say here.

But it wasn't the end of me. It wasn't the end of good gifts. It wasn't the end of God's faithfulness or goodness in my life.

On a Friday in July 2012, my supervisor called a meeting over breakfast. After a few pleasantries, he asked, "Would you be interested in becoming managing editor of the print magazine?" Stunned, I said yes right away. Over eggs, I was invited to take on the most exciting and challenging task of my professional life: I would go on to become the youngest, and first woman, managing editor of the magazine.

Over sandwiches a few hours later, I listened to my then-fiancé read a letter explaining that we would not be getting married, that our conflicts were irresolvable, that we were not meant to live life together. And so it was.

It has taken time for me to understand the significance of that day, of two of my biggest life events unfolding sometime between breakfast and lunch. I probably won't ever totally grasp its meaning. The job offer helped me absorb the blow to my ego that a breakup delivers to most people. On a practical level, it gave me a channel for my time and energy, both of which I had more of once the engagement was over. It gave me a new understanding of Providence: that provision doesn't always come on our timetable, but that God delights in giving his children good gifts, including good work to do.

The broken engagement also challenged my previous assumptions about adulthood and Christian maturity. As it turns out, I was and am responsible for making the most of the time God has given me in this life, with or without a spouse. My life would not have started on my wedding day; my life did not end on the day I learned there would be no wedding day. Marriage is a real and good desire, and it remains one of my own. But it is neither the capstone of maturity nor the scope of God's purposes for his followers.

"Your life doesn't start the day you get married," a friend said to me, shortly after getting married herself. Before meeting Karl Krispin through a friend at age thirty-six, Christy Tennant had led worship music, acted in Virginia and New York City, worked as the executive assistant to the president of Estée Lauder, and advocated for the arts with the International Arts Movement, founded by Makoto Fujimura. In those years, she said, she didn't think about marriage that much. Christy has been my living icon for "making the most of every opportunity, because the days are evil" (Eph. 5:16). (She also has a remarkable ability to learn the life stories of waitstaff—but that's for another book.)

Similarly, says Ashley Elizabeth Graham, "I am convicted by the sense that we will all have to give an account for how we used our talents, for not leaving them wasted." Before leading communications for Tennesseans for Student Success in Nashville, Ashley was a political aide and speechwriter for U.S. Congressman Marsha Blackburn. In that realm, Ashley often felt overlooked by men (usually of an older generation) who would turn to her boyfriend to talk policy before turning to her. Three years ago, she converted to Catholicism, because "the Catholic tradition has a much better framework for single women's vocation than evangelicals do."

Another Family Tree

One helpful thing for us all—married and single—is to look carefully at the arc of Scripture. In the movement from the Old Testament to the New, we see a word of promise spoken over the "stumps."

For Israel, as for most cultures throughout history, marriage and procreation were the focus of community life and ensured the continuation of the family after death. Scripture's long genealogies and mournful accounts of barren women reveal that the family lineage provided the means and stage of God's covenant and promises. But even the Old Testament includes hints of another promise: Eunuchs, barren women, and others who are excluded from Israel's lineage will be given "an everlasting name which will not be cut off . . . a name better than that of sons and daughters" (Isa. 56:1–7). Isaiah 53 in particular speaks of the Messiah's "offspring"—a striking word for someone who never had children!

Jesus' very life and ministry challenge the notion that marriage and family are the primary stage for God's promises and purposes. Or, rather, the central marriage becomes the marriage of Christ and his bride, the church. And the central family becomes the family of all those who call God *Abba* through the Spirit. Jesus regularly used familial language for his followers and rebuked those who would place loyalty to family above loyalty to him (Matt. 12:47–50; Luke 18:29–30). "While the biological family is ultimately temporary in nature, Jesus created in his disciples a new family—the church—that would endure for eternity," writes Al Hsu in the now classic book *Singles at the Crossroads*. In other words, all of our family trees will someday reach an end. But there is another tree whose branches stretch on and on.

And though this is true some days more than others, I can look at a family tree like Shelly's without fear. In Christ, I am not a stump, I am not left barren and bereft, I am not forgotten to history, because in him there is a family tree I belong to, whose branches are anyone who calls on his name in faith. In him my life bears fruit, and in the coming kingdom, in its upside-down way, more are the children of the desolate woman than of her who has a husband (Is. 54).

Katie Nienow

*K*atie Nienow describes her perfect job as a "marriage"—though not to a man.

The Virginia native had worked in Richmond for three years for Young Life, a ministry for suburban teens, when she heard about job openings at HOPE International. The microfinance nonprofit was looking for hires who had "the head of a banker, the heart of a missionary, and the soul of a development worker." In other words, people who loved systems, loved other people, and loved improving the lives of the vulnerable.

"The things I loved about being involved in Young Life, together with the things that I wasn't using, all married together with moving abroad and living in another culture—it felt like a dream come true," says Nienow, thirty-six. She moved to Lubumbashi, a mining city in the Congo, to supervise a bank for three years, then became HOPE's director of development. During her tenure, HOPE grew its fund-raising team from three to ten, doubled its donor base, and increased yearly revenue by 13 percent.

Katie's knack for capital was something she discovered in college. In classes for an economics degree at the University of Virginia, "I remember suddenly feeling like I had found the subject my brain was made to learn and to know."

She wasn't always encouraged to follow that spark.

When she left Young Life for microfinance, her boss said, "You are leaving the one thing God best designed you to do." Even though Katie thought he was wrong, she says, the comment was "devastating." "People believe this is the *thing,* and that nothing else could be higher." It's an implicit hierarchy in Christian communities that see certain kinds of work as more spiritual than others—and anything involving money as belonging on a lower rung.

Today, Katie is confident she is where she's supposed to be, leading a for-profit business. Juntos Finanzas is a technology start-up founded in 2010 to serve the "cash-preferred," a term for people who don't have access to traditional banking. It describes about one in four homes in the United States and nearly half of all U.S. Latino families. While studying at Stanford, co-founder Ben Knelman heard stories from janitors who worked the night shift and wanted to save money but couldn't seem to. He suggested that they start keeping a log of expenses. The simple pen-and-paper system worked, giving the janitors more control over their finances and lives. That inspired Knelman to create a tech-based personal finance tool for cell phone users. Two years in, he invited Katie to join his business as vice president of business development.

Ben, she says, "felt compelled to design products for people who no one else is designing products for. . . . It feels to him very unfair that maybe ninety percent of the world's smart minds are trying to design

what new app to put on our phones to help us order food faster." But Juntos Finanzas' approach is rooted in business, not charity, aimed at equipping users to provide for their families and grow their own businesses. It's the difference between a handout and a hand-up.

Today, with fourteen staff members, Juntos Finanzas stands out in Silicon Valley, where tech companies are notoriously male-dominated. Juntos Finanzas has an equal male-gender ratio, and its board is two women and one man. "We have a particular focus on . . . ensuring that we are sourcing quality female candidates and then hiring the best person," says Katie. One benefit of being a start-up is that leaders can create the work culture as they go; Katie and Ben are intentional about keeping qualified women on who choose to have children. Still, Katie finds, female staff are less likely than male staff to ask for raises. And they are more likely to feel they can't make it in business "when they are not really strong, really well-spoken TJs ["thinking" and "judging" on the Myers-Briggs type indicator]."

Even so, Katie wouldn't describe herself as a "career woman." "My career has actually never felt primary to me," she tells me as we sip tea on a sunny afternoon in Palo Alto. I'm surprised to hear this. "What has felt primary to you?" I ask. *Life.* She goes on:

> It's more holistic. It feels like friends and creativity. I love that my job is part of those things, that I get to have relationships there

and express my gifts there. . . . One of my parallel female Christian friends has been really successful in her career. She also would like to get married, but she's been grateful that her career has felt primary. To me, it never has. It has always felt like a beautiful thing, a fun thing.

For the longest time on my résumé was the Frederick Buechner quote: "My calling is the place where my greatest gifts and the world's greatest needs overlap." I have felt a very strong sense of purpose around that. And yet I've not been very intentional about a career.

Katie also says that she would love to have a family, to "stay home and raise my kids at some point." In the meantime, she is following the marriage of her head, heart, and soul to run a business to the glory of God— and benefit her neighbors in the process.

CHAPTER EIGHT

Embracing Ambition

One of the most ambitious women I have known used to drive a pink pickup truck covered in flowers, with MISS TEA PARTY painted across its flanks. It must have been the girliest Ford F150 to have graced the highways of Henrico County, Virginia.

Kim Newlen was a South Carolina native who had a penchant for adding the word "sweet" before everyone's names. In 1995, the stay-at-home mother was itching for purpose and friendship. So she began hosting women in her Virginia home. The slogan—"Women's Social on a Shoestring . . . Tied to a Generous God"—promised an unpretentious gathering for women rooted in simple spiritual principles.

Newlen's monthly gatherings quickly took off, and soon she launched Sweet Monday, an evangelistic ministry that eventually expanded to homes and college campuses in every state. In 2005, Newlen broke the Guinness World Record for World's Largest Tea Party, hosting more than seven thousand people on the campus of the University of Richmond. (The record has since been smashed by the residents of Summerville, South Carolina, who love their sweet tea.) Many of the attendees wore pink.

Who knows how many of the tea drinkers that day were aware that Newlen was walking the campus battling one of the most aggressive forms of breast cancer. The year prior, at age forty-seven, Newlen had undergone a lumpectomy, radiation, a full mastectomy . . . then full chemotherapy . . . then full radiation: "every complication that can occur with cancer short of death," she said.

Quite naturally, Kim told *Christianity Today* in a 2012 documentary film, "I thought what I would do was just pull the covers over my head and wait until everything was over." Instead, "the exact opposite happened. No one could have been more surprised than me . . . that I would have gotten bolder as I got balder, but I did."

After Newlen had endured every skirmish in her battle against cancer, she realized that one of her greatest needs during her endless hospital visits and treatments was a dose of normalcy. For many women enduring breast cancer, that means going about feminine routines of beauty and personal care. Working with a fashion designer based in Manhattan, Newlen created and patented a special postsurgical garment for women who have to wear drains that remove fluid from the surgery. Today, the Look Better Than You Feel™ garment is used in hospitals throughout Virginia, offering women dignity during a life experience that brings anything but.

"I've always wanted to be a woman who didn't live with regret," Newlen told *CT*. "Life is so short, I didn't want to look back and say, *I wish I had, I wish I had.*"

Ambition is refusing to say, "I wish I had."

"Make a Name for Ourselves"

Since the word first appeared in the fourteenth century, ambition has gotten a universally bad rap. Related to the word "amble," it used to conjure someone going from town to town to get votes or support. Ambition is bad because it is almost always associated with the self. Wherever ambition is, ego, praise, and pride seem to lie close at hand.

History and popular culture give us many examples of the wreckage of ambition. Ambition is Lady Macbeth whispering to her husband to commit murder. Ambition is the thousands of executives, investors, and analysts who promised that certain financial institutions were "too big to fail," then watched the global economy crash in 2008. Ambition is Napoleon at Waterloo. Ambition is *House of Cards'* Frank Underwood. Ambition is Tonya Harding.

You'll recall King Leopold of Belgium, whom we met in Chapter 1 and who ruled over Congo from 1885 to 1908. It would be an understatement to say that Leopold had ambitions in the way any man of nineteenth-century Europe had ambitions. The eldest son of Belgium's king at the height of colonialist rule, Leopold was practically born with ambition coursing through his veins. To rule, to expand, to make great the name of his relatively small country—this was the way of life that Leopold II of Belgium had inherited.

It was ambition that led Leopold to get license from other European countries in 1885 to take the Congo Free State, ostensibly to Christianize its inhabitants. It was also ambition that drove him to establish massive labor camps to harvest rubber and ivory by force of military power; to erect buildings and parks throughout Belgium, earning him the epithet "Builder King" (instead of, say, "Genocidal Crazy"). And it was ultimately ambition that blinded him to the exploitation and violence that took an estimated ten million Congolese lives.

Christianity traditionally has less than friendly things to say about ambition. In his *Confessions*, Augustine of Hippo, the great fourth-century theologian, calls "worldly ambition" (*ambitio saeculi*) the single greatest enemy of the well-lived life. Thomas Aquinas warned of "the immoderate or inordinate desire for honor." And the theologians of the Protestant Reformation weren't much friendlier; in the words of John Calvin:

> Ambition deludes men so much that by its sweetness it not only intoxicates but drives them mad— and doubtless, ambition not only does injury to men, but exalts itself even against God.

Such warnings make sense. We follow a Savior who cast off "honor or preferment," with "nothing in his appearance that we should desire him" (Isa. 53:2). Jesus of Nazareth— the only human innately entitled to honor and majesty and praise from the ones who populate the earth he created— relinquished his claim to them, instead taking on the nature of a servant (Phil. 2:7). The God of the universe is not so haughty as to give up the claims to prestige. So why would we, sinful, frail creatures we are, have any right not to do the same?

From the biblical perspective, under the power of sin, ambition is defined as humans striving to be like God apart from the power of God. And apart from God, ambition only ends badly—if not in financial or legal ruin, then in the warping of the soul ever toward the self.

From the earliest pages of Scripture, we learn of the damage incurred when humans try to be like God without submitting to God. In Genesis 11, we learn that early human communities vowed to "make a name for ourselves," scheming to build "a tower that reaches to the heavens." The Tower of Babel is a cautionary tale of what happens when we erect a career, a reputation, or a "platform" without first submitting our desires and efforts to God. When we try to build our own "towers," we bring to ourselves and others confusion, chaos, and a loss of security, which is often the very thing we seek as we set about our tower-making plans.

In fact, the problem with the Tower of Babel was that its builders' ambitions were too small. As Andy Crouch notes in *Playing God: Redeeming the Gift of Power*, "The bravado of Babel conceals an undercurrent of fear; this seemingly ambitious building project is actually the result of diminished human ambition and a growing human sense of vulnerability."

You read that right: The story of Babel provides a lesson about the danger of having too *little* ambition. Babel's citizens weren't dreaming big enough; they could see only their insecurity and fear that they "shall be scattered abroad upon the face of the whole earth." From an eternal perspective, their ambitions were not too big but too small. The fears that usually drive us to ambition—fear of losing power, of losing face, of losing life—often come true when we fail to submit our fears to God.

But ambition was always a part of what God intended for his image bearers, male and female. God doesn't want to kill your ambition; he wants to use it for his—and your—good.

Our Ambitious Savior

Here is how Carolyn Custis James describes it in her best-selling book, *Half the Church: Recapturing God's Global Vision for Women:*

> God . . . didn't create a flat earth. God's world has mountains that awaken in us the need to climb, to test our limits and find out firsthand what it's like to stand atop a snowy peak. He created a world that is packed with endless treasure, raw material, and unexplored frontiers designed to stir up in us the artist, the scientist, the explorer-adventurer, the athlete, the mathematician, the botanist, the entrepreneur, and much more.
>
> Mountains cry out to be climbed. Dirt says to us, "Dig." The ocean's fathomless waters invite us to go on a deep-sea treasure hunt. The heavens declare not only the glory of God; they also declare that we were made to test their bounds and marvel at their beauty.
>
> This is true for every sphere of creation and of human culture: God made all of us, male and female, to explore the world he created, to know it, care for it, and have dominion over it for his glory and others' benefit. God's original creation was good yet latent with potential. It was

pristine yet incomplete. Missing were the work, curiosity, and energy of humans, the only part of the creation bearing the image of God. Human ambition wasn't something that crept in after the Fall. It was—is—an aspect of bearing the image of God, of filling his world with beauty and industry and delight.

Ambition leaves a sour taste on the tongue of many a Christian. And rightly so: For eight years, I have edited a magazine that covers news and trends in Christendom, and I can say that the worst news about Christian leaders and communities seems to center on ambition gone bad. The fallen pastor, the collapsing church, the insolvent ministry— outsize ambition and a hefty dose of hubris are always intertwined in a larger tangle of sin that capsizes the best intentions.

But consider that the most ambitious person who ever walked the earth is Jesus. Christ lived with a crystal-clear will and one orienting desire: "to do the will of him who sent me and to finish his work" (John 4:34). There was nothing passive or happenstance about Jesus' ministry. He had a pure and powerful inward will: to preach the gospel of salvation, to heal the sick, to raise the dead, to be a stumbling block to the haughty and powerful, and to take up the cross in all its crushing weight to accomplish his most important work of atoning for the sins of the world.

This is the type of ambition that we Christians are to have, by God's grace, no matter our stage of life or spheres of influence. Oriented toward God, *ambition is the setting of the will to accomplish the desire of the heart*. It is the motor that keeps us pressing for shalom, for hints of his kingdom to appear in our offices and schools and city halls and homes. Ambition is the choice to continue pursuing God's will be done when our energies and passions are sapped. For Christians to live as the *tsaddiqim* on the earth, they need the doggedness, vision, and shrewdness that are marks of people who shape and lead our society in profound ways.

It's the type of ambition exemplified by Alice Seeley Harris, whom we met in Chapter 1. Especially considering her cultural milieu and its beliefs about separate spheres, Harris never would have ended up in the Congo without a healthy dose of ambition.

It took ambition for Harris to leave her family behind in Malmesbury, England, to enter the Civil Service at age nineteen. It took ambition for her to travel by boat, then by foot, to a mission station in a remote jungle village to begin teaching children four days after her wedding. Ambition is ultimately why Harris kept advocating for the Congolese and the end of Leopold's rule, to take her photos on tour throughout England and the United States, to keep publishing pamphlets and books providing bald evidence of the devastation left by someone else's ungodly ambitions.

However, if ambition is a hard virtue for Christians to grasp, it is doubly hard for Christian women.

Getting Over Selfish Ambition

Here is how Linda Beail remembers it. Beail is a political scientist at Point Loma Nazarene University, where she directs a women's studies center. (She also coauthored a book with one of the best alliterations I've ever seen: *Framing Sarah Palin: Pit Bulls, Puritans, and Politics*.) She writes, "When I was growing up, I heard a lot about the importance of 'finding God's will for your life' . . . I desperately wanted to know what God was calling me to do."[34] At the same time:

> I never heard people talk about how much they loved and admired their mothers for being so ambitious; when I heard family, friends, or even celebrities and politicians praising their wives and mothers, it was for being so caring, nurturing of others, and self-sacrificing. "Ambition" seemed cold and self-centered in comparison.

Sadly, this gives women false choices in identity formation. You can be either nurturing and self-sacrificing *or* ambitious. But Jesus—and many saints of history who set the world on fire for God—dismantles that false dichotomy. We can be self-giving and self-driven, content with our circumstances, yet deeply discontent when those circumstances are filled with suffering and injustice. Rather than dismissing ambition outright, we need to ask what ends our ambitions serve and amplify those ambitions when they serve good, holy ends.

According to Beail, questions of vocation for women go beyond a specific line of work, or the false dichotomy of professional work versus domestic work, to deeper questions of identity: *Who am I? What was I made to do, and how*

---

34. Beail, Linda, and Sylvia Cortez Masyuk, eds. "The Importance of Ambition for Christian Women: Participating in God's Work in the World," in *Results May Vary* (San Diego: Point Loma Press, 2013), page 113.

do I know? From an early age, many women have these questions answered for them. Because women's identities have, historically speaking, been so essentially tied to being a wife and mother, many Christian women today feel guilty for having ambitions beyond that. "If we seek meaningful work, success, or power, must we do it only for the benefit of others—not admitting our own need for affirmation and worth?" writes Beail.

Sheryl Sandberg begins *Lean In* by describing the "leadership ambition gap" she has observed between men and women. Growing up, she posits, girls and boys receive different messages about the relative value of striving for professional success. "'She is *very* ambitious' is not a compliment in our culture," writes Sandberg, noting that women who are hard-charging often pay a social cost, earning a reputation for being "pushy" or "intimidating." Women who do reach the highest levels of corporate influence often struggle with the feeling that they are impostors. Or they attribute their success to luck or being in the right place at the right time.

Mothers of young children in particular can struggle to admit or express their aspirations beyond motherhood. Because their minds and bodies are so oriented toward others who depend on them in those early years, it can seem selfish or sinful to want something for themselves.

The pressures are both internal and external. Strong cultural norms constrain the types of self-oriented activities appropriate for women with kids at home. A pampering day at a women's retreat? A trip to L.A. Nails? Go ahead! In the words of Donna Meagle and Tom Haverford on *Parks and Recreation,* treat yo'self!

But move your family across the country for a tenure-track teaching position? Spend a week alone at a writing retreat or conference? It varies by subculture and location and husband. But the latter examples of seemingly self-oriented choices are much harder sells, perhaps for the very women who most want them.

"I know many women who assume 'mommy guilt' is a way of life," writes Diane Paddison, founder and president of 4Word Women. "Even (and in some cases especially) my Christian friends accept this extreme burden of guilt, shame, and self-doubt as part of the universal motherhood experience." Tish Harrison Warren, whom we heard from in Chapter 6, says she internalized this kind of guilt growing up. "When I work outside the home, I feel like my husband is doing me a favor," she said. She assured me that her husband does not think of it as a favor, and "that is a great gift," says Tish. "But I don't want to feel like an ambitious wife is a burden."

I don't want to feel like a burden. Try to imagine a man saying this—especially about his career—and it's almost humorous. Try to imagine a woman saying it, and it seems like a mantra of femininity.

Yet I wonder if some Christian women avoid the crucial questions of ambition—*What is my heart's desire? In what direction do I set my will?*—because they don't know how they would answer them. Family, friendships, and others-oriented ministry become culturally acceptable ways to avoid a deeper ambiguity about who they are and what they are made to do.

As Baeil notes, our very notions of sin are *gendered,*

meaning that men and women are prone to embody sinful-
ness in ways that are distinct to maleness and femaleness.
As such, writes Baeil, "Women . . . may because of their social experiences be far less likely to become prideful and
selfish [than men], but more likely to fall into the sin of
idolizing relationships." In other words, placing others at
the center of our lives can be just as wrong as placing ourselves as the center of our lives. Either way, God is not at
the center, and for that we are less able to hear his distinct
call upon our lives.

"But seek first the kingdom of God and His righteousness, and all these things will be provided for you" (Matt.
6:33). For many Christian women, this seeking *will* mean
investing a large portion of their lives in caring for others.
Of course, women should not trade selflessness for *selfish-
ness*. Rather, it's that seeking the kingdom of God is an invitation for all disciples of Christ, and that to ignore the
invitation is to ignore the joy and fulfillment to be found in
living on mission for the glory of God.

A Real Go-getter

When I was in junior high school, my friend Lauren started
getting paid to get good grades. If she earned a C on a test,
her parents would give her five dollars. If she earned a B,
the rate would double. An A was worth a whopping twenty
dollars—enough to buy the new Spice Girls album and a
pair of earrings at Claire's.

I remember this arrangement not only because it made

Lauren's parents seem infinitively cooler than mine but also because, by comparison, I didn't need rewards for good grades; getting an A *was* my reward. This was true for many of my activities: piano, Girl Scouts, marching band, youth group. Whatever I was doing, I wanted to do it with excellence.

My grandparents had these little sayings that they would repeat when we visited them every month or so in Cincinnati, Ohio. "That Kate—she's sure going places!" they would say, or "Kate's a real go-getter." I always felt Granny and Boompa's pride, yet I also knew that their love was unconditional. That combination was a great early gift to me.

As I have grown up, my "natural" ambition has at times proved to be a double-edged sword. I will never forget how difficult it was to nod politely as a woman several years older than I am—the leader of a prominent singles ministry—began offering advice about how I should approach my career in light of other desires. She told me she had spent her twenties and thirties pouring a lot into her career, assuming that marriage and family would come along in due time. She offered her own story to warn me about what can happen when a Christian invests too much in her work and too little in finding a spouse. It was a bad case of womansplaining.

After our chat, I wondered how I might practically implement this ministry leader's advice. Spending as much time and energy finding a husband as editing a magazine seemed a form of poor stewardship, not to mention an exhausting and frustrating way to live. Besides, many Christian communities discourage women from pursuing men in the first place.

Perhaps this ministry leader meant that I could be ambitious but shouldn't *appear* to be, lest it seem like I was too busy to fit a relationship into my life. Others have suggested that men find me intimidating—a compliment that takes even as it gives. While at times I have wondered if I need to play down my aspirations or not talk so much about work, most days I conclude, alongside Nigerian writer Chimamanda Ngozi Adichie, that "a man who would be intimidated by me is exactly the kind of man I would have no interest in."

Because of my ambitious bent, contentment has *not* always come naturally to me. To this day, when I hear Christians talk about finding contentment, I bristle. It sounds too much like settling, like refusing to show up to the challenge and invitation of life before God.

Mainstream culture has too often offered women an ambition made in men's image: to build our own little professional kingdoms, with enough left over for bigger homes and more lavish vacations and more manicured social-media feeds. Secular ambition rightly invites women to make the most of every opportunity but for completely wrong ends: for material gain and our own name's sake.

By contrast, Christian culture has too often offered women a push toward contentment that can numb us to our own desires, without offering the tools to discern whether those desires could be good or Holy Spirit–inspired. As Jen Pollock Michel explored beautifully in her book *Teach Us to*

Want, many Christians have learned to mistrust or tamp down longings because they might create discontent. For example, one women's devotional from 2008 starts this way:

> Our unhappiness does not spring from what we lack. It springs from our *desire* for what we lack. . . . We crave the smooth rhythm of a balanced life—a little of this, a bit of that, but not too much for either. We are unhappy because we have come to expect such things, living as we do in a society that advocates personal rights, autonomy, and prosperity above all else.

In other words, the root of our discontent is desire. So for us to be truly happy in Christ, we must pluck out the weed of desire.

To be sure, in the privileged West, many of us *are* glutted with endless consumer choices, yet are taunted by comparisons to others who have better jobs, cuter babies, trimmer bodies, and bigger budgets. There is much beauty and countercultural witness in living knowing that God has given us enough for today, that he is our strength and portion forever (Ps. 73:26).

But the problem facing most Christian women isn't desire for "personal rights, autonomy, and prosperity above all else." We are not discontent because we cannot achieve that elusive balance, language that every woman I spoke with found unhelpful. We are not discontent because we desire, for to live and breathe is to desire; humans are, in the words of one Christian philosopher, "desiring agents."

Rather, I wonder if we are discontent because we have

ambitions but don't know how to express them or realize them. We desire many good things yet don't know how to humanly pursue them given our mortality. Our good ambitions bump up against our real, embodied limitations. Thankfully, Christ, the most ambitious person who ever lived, also embraced a life of limits.

Embracing Our Limits

Less than two years after *Christianity Today* created a short film about her, Kim Newlen succumbed to cancer, dying peacefully in the winter of 2014. She was remembered as a loving wife, mother, friend, ministry partner, and entrepreneur—someone who took the pain and humiliation of an unforgiving disease and created from it tremendous good. Who added to the world a material good that no man likely could or would have invented. Faced with disease and death, Newlen made the most of her limitations, ensuring that she wouldn't say "I wish I had."

Not many of us will endure the physical suffering that Newlen did, thank goodness. But one way or another, all of us will face the limits of embodied human life. Our ambitions—even the ones we believe are from God—will crash upon the shores of our finitude. We will want to be in two places at the same time and will have to say no to one. We will want to take the job offer at just the moment when a family member falls ill. We will want to get pregnant at the moment when we're invited to a long-term missions post in a country with poor medical care. We will want to write a novel but have three young children at home. Those of us for whom ambition comes naturally will have to say no to many good offers because they are not where God is leading.

All of us have to eat and sleep to live. All of us will need a weekly Sabbath. And very few of us will see all of our dreams realized in our own lifetimes. Death is the great equalizer.

However, our own limitations need not kill our ambition or lull us to passively accept whatever happens. Rather, our limitations can clarify the godly tasks we are to pursue with our limited time on earth. With Christ as our model, our limitations are the very foundation upon which true ambition rests.

Few people I know have written as much or as well on the beauty of constraints as Kate Harris. Until recently the executive director of the Washington Institute for Faith, Vocation, and Culture, Harris notes that God himself willingly took on constraints in the person of Christ. The Incarnation is a radical claim of the Christian faith because it attests to a God who stoops down low to the world of limitations. The ruler of the universe, in Jesus Christ, binds himself to a particular time and place, to specific people and circumstances, and ultimately, to the risk of weariness and sickness of human flesh.[35] "[God] chose to work through the same ordinary human constraints we all face—he did not see these as impediments but rather as the purpose," writes Harris.

---

35. Harris writes more about constraints in the book *Wonder Women: Navigating the Challenges of Motherhood, Career, and Identity* (Grand Rapids, MI: Barna Frames, 2014).

In Christ, God chose the greatest of human limitations and wrought from that the highest of enterprises: to rescue humanity from the power of sin and death, and to win for all who believe new and unending life in him.

This means that God knows our every limitation from the inside out (Heb. 4:15). It also means he can use our limitations to accomplish his purposes on earth. My theology would hesitate to say that God "gave" Kim Newlen cancer. But it's clear that God used the scourge of cancer to plant in her a creativity and self-giving love that blooms to this day. If he can use the cross to accomplish her purposes on earth, he can certainly use our limitations to do the same.

The ambition God invites us to is a cross-shaped ambition: to embrace our inability to have it all so that he may be our all. Likewise, the contentment to which God invites us is a cross-shaped contentment: to *choose* to say "thy will be done," to willingly embrace our own constraints, because it is often through human weakness that God most clearly displays his power and glory.

Until God is our all in all, may we be bold enough to hold on to our ambitions, to keep turning them in the light to see what holy and surprising refractions bounce back. To be vulnerably honest before God about what we want and why we want, then to step back and see what he will do. To be content with his answer but to let even a "no" be the grounds for fruitfulness within constraints. To allow our disappointments and the frustration of our dreams become the seedbed of deeper trust in the Lord of the universe and the Lord of our lives.

Whatever we do—in our workplaces, in our homes and neighborhoods, in the highest and lowest realms of culture—may we work at it with all our hearts, knowing that it is God, not man, whom we serve. It is God, not man, who calls us to reign.

Mitali Perkins

*O*f the ten books that Mitali Perkins has written for children and young teenagers, several of them center on "the hyphenated life."

Perkins was born in Kolkata, India, the daughter of Hindu parents who were in an arranged marriage. On account of her father's career as a civil engineer, Mitali and her family had lived in Ghana, Cameroon, London, New York City, Mexico, and finally, California by the time she was age eleven. In all of these places, she said, her family never totally adapted to the culture, retaining the customs and language of their Bengali background.

Given the culture's rich literary tradition, Mitali's father instilled in his children a love for storytelling and used his Saturdays off to collect novels for Mitali from the library. Always in but never of the place where her family lived, Mitali gravitated to books to provide a sense of home. Prince Edward Island, the backdrop for L. M. Montgomery's beloved *Anne of Green Gables,* became a type of home; so did Concord, Massachusetts, the setting of Meg, Jo, Beth, and Amy March's sisterhood in Louisa May Alcott's *Little Women.* "Stories were my lifeline, my rock, my stability," said Mitali. "They were what I clutched for balance in that sometimes confusing place between cultures."

Without her realizing it at the time, stories also provided an early exposure to the gospel. *"A Little Princess*

and *The Secret Garden*—all of them have threads of the redemptive work of Christ," Mitali told me. "It was almost like I was being spiritually mothered through these books and spiritually fathered through Tolkien and Lewis." Later, as a nineteen-year-old political science major at Stanford University, Mitali was encouraged by a friend to read the Bible. Without any overt exposure to the Scriptures, she read them primarily as a story, not a theological tome. "Jesus is magnetic," she said. "As a writer, you realize he was a very surprising character, and he was also very Middle Eastern, not a white guy." Mitali later chose Jesus to be her "guru," then gave her life to him through the InterVarsity Christian Fellowship group on Stanford's campus.

Today, Mitali, 52, writes stories about young people living "between cultures" or on the margins of society. Her first novel, *The Sunita Experiment,* was the winning entry in a contest sponsored by Little, Brown. Her second, *Monsoon Summer,* had a more difficult entry into the literary world; it was rejected twenty-three times and published, finally, by Random House eleven years after *The Sunita Experiment.* In that time, Mitali married a pastor, lived in Thailand, India, and Bangladesh, and became a mom to twins adopted from India. At four months, the boys weighed just 6 pounds, so "motherhood became an all-consuming vocational call."

Mitali says her heart for justice became very particular with their adoption. "I had these big, wide calls to care for the poor, and God made that call very

particular. He gave me a wider impact than my plan of how I was going to change the world. Embracing the call to motherhood meant embracing the insignificant and being invisible."

God did not forget Mitali's love of storytelling even while she was raising the boys. In 2006, she had the opportunity to pursue a Ph.D.; she also had an offer to work with homeless communities in Santa Monica. On a one-day spiritual retreat to ask God what she should do, she went down to the Catholic retreat center's musty library and pulled out an obscure book titled *The Spiritual Vocation of Writing for Children.* Mitali pored over the book—as clear a sign as any, she said, that she should pursue writing novels as a profession, treating it with the same devotion and standards of excellence that she would any other full-time job.

And the investment has paid off. Her fifth novel, *Rickshaw Girl*, centers on Naima, a ten-year-old Bangladeshi who disguises herself as a boy in order to work in her father's rickshaw business. It was named one of the best 100 children's books of the past century by the New York Public Library, is being made into a feature-length film, and was adapted for the stage by the Bay Area Children's Theater. Her first picture book releases in 2018 and is set along the fence between Mexico and California. And at the time of this writing, she had just signed a six-figure contract for two novels, the first of which explores the gains and losses of a hyphenated life.

Mitali says her husband's Christ-centered preaching, as well as her "vocational life verses" (Philippians 2, which includes the command to "do nothing out of selfish ambition or vain conceit"), keep her grounded. "Battling selfish ambition and vain conceit is a discouraging, dark part of the writing life," she says. "These verses remind me to keep my eyes on those who don't have a voice."

Where Do We Go from Here

How All of Us Can Equip Women for Work

In the late 1970s, when Katherine Leary Alsdorf was in her mid-twenties, she found herself working on the U.S. Space Shuttle Program. The New Jersey native had always wanted to be an elementary school teacher. But after working one summer at an aerospace economics firm, she realized there was a world out there beyond the classroom. She worked her way up from an entry-level position in New Jersey to managing the Shuttle project from California.

During that time, Katherine embarked on her first business trip with a client. The two were having dinner together, and soon a waitress arrived at the table. She was wearing a miniskirt and a top "down to here," said Katherine, pointing somewhere many inches below the neckline. The client talked with the waitress far longer than was necessary for ordering dinner. After she left, he turned to Katherine.

"See her? She's a fox," he said. "And you? You gotta make up your mind. Are you going to be a businesswoman or a fox? Because right now, you're trying to do both, and you're not doing very well at either."

That night, Katherine went back to her hotel room, thinking about the choice her client had presented. Was she going to be a businesswoman, or a "fox"? As she had to go earn her pay, the next morning she put her hair in a bun and decided: *I'm going to be a businesswoman.*

And she was, with great success. After earning an MBA, Katherine moved to New York City, where she was asked to take over as president/CEO of a technology startup when the former president/CEO stepped down amid a medical emergency. She later became CEO of two tech startups in Silicon Valley, leading teams of mostly men as a single woman and as a Christian. She had come to Christ after a friend prodded her to attend Redeemer Presbyterian Church. A decade and several companies later, lead pastor Timothy Keller would ask her to create the Center for Faith and Work. It is now twelve years old.

In the thirty-five years since Katherine had that fateful dinner with her client, American business culture has sufficiently changed such that many women would, in fact, rather be known for being businesswomen than for being foxes. The rate of women entering the workforce has risen steadily since 1979, to about six in ten U.S. women currently working. Many of these jobs are in professions long thought to be better fit for men. According to journalist Hanna Rosin, for every two men who receive a degree in business this year, three women will do the same. The *Economist* reports that women have added more value to the global GDP than new technology or emerging markets in India and China combined!

But in other ways, our culture has not caught up with

the fact that most women want to and indeed do work. We all know the sobering headlines: Women are still paid less than men for performing the same work. Mothers face inflexible leave policies, a perception of incompetence ("mommy brain"), and across-the-board lower pay than even their childless female peers. And while women today have more recourse against sexual harassment than Katherine did, they still face it. It's just less likely to be a client advising you on your appearance, and more likely to be insidious forms of gender discrimination.

And, most important for our purposes, the body of Christ has not responded well to the Katherines coming through our doors and growing up in our midst.

"A Challenging, Pioneering Time"

I started this book with two claims at once unremarkable and provocative: One, every human being is made to work. Two, since women are human beings, every woman is made to work.

Up to this point, this book has been directed at women—the God-given goodness they can find in work; the challenges they face as they integrate professions with motherhood; the ambitions they bring before God even as they learn to live within embodied limitations; and much more. I hope that women will read this book and talk to each other about it a lot.

But no human being, male or female, works alone. Regardless of the type of professional work, we all must labor alongside others in order to be effective and fruitful. The teacher must have students. The fashion designer must have a seamstress and a tailor and a client or two. The president of a company must have a board. To paraphrase John Donne, no worker is an island entire of herself.

No human being works alone in another, spiritual sense: We discover the deep meaning of our work only when it is placed within the larger story of God's work in the world. Because we Christians have so many competing narratives about work—that it's primarily about financial gain, that it requires taking down others, that it is our key source of value—we need to hear and rehear the Christian narrative about our nine-to-five life.

For that, we need a community of people who can reflect back to us work's true meaning and purpose. Christians have such a community built in: the local church. But in a time when women show no signs of exiting the workforce, and in fact are outpacing men in many sectors, many churches continue to understand and frame work as only or predominantly a men's issue.

There are many reasons for this. One is that some church leaders still aren't talking about work, period. Or when they do, secular work is framed as less important than the work done in a church building. This was the attitude that Tom Nelson, a pastor in Kansas City, admits he held for years. In an interview for a *Christianity Today* video series, Nelson says he repented of holding a sub-biblical view of his members' professional work:

> I have spent the majority of my time and teaching
> equipping you for what you're called to do in the

minority of your life. I've completely ignored to my fault and to your peril and to the gospel's richness what you're called to do the majority of your life. I've equipped you for just a Sunday Christian. And from this day, our team, we're going to change.

In other words, Nelson recognized that most of his members spent most of their time, week in and week out, at their jobs, and thus need to know how to think about that work Christianly.

It seems more pastors are following his lead. A recent Barna Group study confirmed that more pastors are talking positively about professional work than even five years ago. In 2014, 86 percent of pastors said they had preached on God's view of work and faith/work integration within the past year; 36 percent said they had done so in the past month. That was up from 2011, when just 26 percent of pastors said they preached on faith and work at all.

Some churches host intensive programs to address the "Sunday-to-Monday gap." Falls Church Anglican—one of the oldest and most vibrant Anglican churches in the country—started its Fellows Program in 1995 to equip college graduates to "live a seamless life of faith." As of 2015, their model had spread to twenty-plus churches across the country, giving more than two hundred young people part-time work, mentoring, Bible study, and community. And beginning in 2003, under Katherine's leadership, the Center for Faith and Work equips and mobilizes believers in their professional lives. Its Gotham Fellowship takes young professionals (ages twenty-four to thirty-four) through a nine-month intensive program "to deepen their experience of the gospel . . . in their work and vocation."

Other churches have followed suit. In 2015, Christ Presbyterian Church launched the Nashville Institute for Faith and Work. There, "those in secular vocations of any kind can be equipped and connected to each other [and] . . . become more effective in their roles as workers in God's story."[36] The Cascade Fellows program convenes members from eight Seattle churches for nine months of connecting faith and work. Ten churches have partnered with the Denver Institute for Faith and Work, founded in 2013, to prepare laypeople to "humbly share the good news of God's grace in and through their work."[37] Such vocational discipleship programs tend to attract men and women in equal measure.

But men's and women's work still isn't addressed from pulpits in equal measure. Women I interviewed for this book said that when their pastors preached on work, they referred to men's work. Molly Sheffield, whom I met in Seattle, has worked in media for twenty-plus years and currently directs an advertising service. She and her husband, Dave, used to be members of a nationally recognized Seattle megachurch. "One of the first sermons I heard from the pulpit was this pastor saying he didn't know any females who worked outside the home," she said. "And here I was, thirty-three or thirty-four years old,

---

36. http://christpres.org/missy-wallace/.

37. http://denverinstitute.org/church-partnership-program/.

and had worked my butt off at advertising agencies in my twenties. I was like, 'Dave, come on. How can he not know that?'"

We might chalk this up to idiosyncratic teachings from this pastor and church. But even in churches where women's gifts are seen and affirmed, there lingers a subtle association between work and men. We are contending with the work/home divide wrought by the Industrial Revolution.

An acquaintance shared with me that, at her Baptist church in Wheaton, Illinois, the faith-and-work programming is formally under the men's ministry. Meanwhile, many churches schedule their women's Bible studies and events during the day. This quietly assumes that women aren't working during the day. Alyssa Hasty, a professor of molecular physiology and biophysics at Vanderbilt University, said, "I know that men's groups often meet early in the morning, but I never hear of women's groups that do that. I know sometimes they meet on Saturday, but that is really hard because I need my Saturdays to catch up on everything that hasn't gotten done during the week."

When she was leading a tech start-up in California, Katherine asked her pastor if she could join the group of CEOs whom he met with on a regular basis. He said, "Well, actually, it's all men, so why don't you go find a group of women CEOs and you can have your own group?"

Katherine wasn't sure why a group focused on leadership out in the world needed to be gender-specific. Further, Katherine didn't know other women CEOs at the church; the women CEOs she knew didn't go to church and probably wouldn't feel welcome if they did. "For most career women in the church, it's been a challenging, pioneering time," she said.

And during this pioneering, challenging time, many Christian women live their lives between the pew and the office feeling disintegrated and confused. Karen Dabaghian, a computer software professional in San Francisco, said, "In high-tech, nobody cares [about your gender]. You could be purple, you could be missing body parts . . . but if you're confident and working hard, there's a place for you." She notes that she's often the only woman at the table of mostly engineers, and this has been to her advantage. "Then I go into this broader Christian environment, and all of a sudden, I feel gendered, in a way that is not something I'm excited about," says Dabaghian, a wife and mother of two. "I find a very strong division between my secular world experience and my Christian world experience."

Lagging Behind

The faith-at-work (FAW) movement arose in the early twentieth century precisely to address the secular/sacred division that Karen describes.

"They might as well have just posted a sign outside the church: 'Corporate types not welcome to worship here.'" David W. Miller, director of the Faith & Work Initiative at Princeton University, begins his definitive book, *God at Work: The History and Promise of the Faith and Work Movement,* with this quote from his friend Steve. Steve had attended a Sunday school class in which his pastor

denounced "the greed of all multinationals" and their executives. The pastor implied that one couldn't be a Christian
at this particular company. At it turns out, Steve, a committed Christian, was that company's chairman and CEO.

Miller begins his history of FAW with this story because
it illustrates poignantly why the movement emerged *beyond*
the walls of the church. FAW is Miller's umbrella term for
theological teaching and "special-purpose groups" that
emerged throughout the twentieth century to minister to lay
Christians, especially businessmen. Over three eras spanning
the 1890s to the present, FAW has aimed to help Christians
see, in the words of Elton Trueblood (an influential theologian in FAW's second era), that all Christians are called to
"full-time Christian work." He wrote that a few Christians

> ought to leave their secular employment in order to
> engage in full-time work for the promotion of the
> gospel [via preaching and evangelism], but this is
> not true of most. Most men ought to stay where
> they are and to make their Christian witness in or-
> dinary work rather than beyond it.[38]

We should take the "men" in Trueblood's statement literally. Miller reports that women were absent from the FAW
movement in its first two waves. "While women emerged as
lay leaders in other early twentieth-century movements . . .
[think of Alice Seeley Harris from Chapter 1], the business
community and professional workplace outside the home
remained largely out of bounds for women," he notes. "The

---

38. Trueblood, Elton. *Your Other Vocation* (New York: Harper & Row, 1952).

absence of prominent females in the movement in waves one and two can probably be attributed to the traditional gender roles assigned to women in society." In other words, the early FAW movement was overwhelmingly male because so few women attained white-collar jobs.

It makes sense that many FAW groups started essentially as men's fellowship groups. One of the largest was the Christian Business Men's Committee (CBMC). It was founded in 1937 in Chicago to encourage businessmen after the Great Depression. Since then, CBMC has rebranded as Connecting Business and the Marketplace to Christ, and today, it claims eighteen thousand members in the United States. While CBMC currently accepts women members and has ties to the smaller Christian Business Women's Fellowship, thirteen of its fourteen board members are men, and all eight of its global leadership team members are men. When I asked CBMC's international offices for the male/female ratio of its members, its ministry coordinator said that they do not keep track of those numbers. "Our focus is not on gender, but on transforming the world by the gospel of Jesus Christ," she wrote.

Likewise, the Fellowship of Companies for Christ International (FCCI), founded in 1977 and based in Atlanta, has made efforts to attract professional women. I asked Terence Chatmon, FCCI's president/CEO, about the male/female ratio of its members and board leadership. Chatmon said in the past four years, FCCI has "been very intentional and proactive to diversify its nonprofit marketplace ministry to reflect more of the society and people who make up the executive leadership in America." Still, 75 to 80 percent of

FCCI's business leadership groups are led by men. And although the board is 40 percent diversified in ethnic terms, all members are male. (Notably, Chatmon told me via email, "I am probably the only African-American leading a major marketplace ministry in the world," underscoring the FAW's ethnic as well as gender homogeneity. More attention needs to be drawn to FAW's racial makeup—in another book! Mark that as the fourth book I'm asking someone else to write.)

CBMC and FCCI are just two of the estimated twelve hundred organizations today that promote faith/work integration.[39] Miller notes that most FAW groups have expanded their membership to women. A few FAW groups are led by women: Tami Heim, president/CEO of the Christian Leadership Alliance (full disclosure, Heim serves on the board of Christianity Today); Lisa Slayton, president of the Pittsburgh Leadership Foundation; and Missy Wallace, executive director of the Nashville Institute for Faith and Work. Further, women-only groups such as Diane Paddison's 4word Women and Women Doing Well—a philanthropy group harnessing Christian women's earning power to charitable causes—meet what Miller calls "a growing demand of many professional women for a confident, sympathetic forum."

But two national women-focused FAW groups hardly seem enough to reach the 74 percent of all adult U.S. women who currently work.

---

39. http://www.calvin.edu/scs/2009/Rundle%20Johnson/; quoted in Sherman, Amy, *Kingdom Calling* (Downers Grove, IL: InterVarsity Press, 2011), page 92.

Amy Sherman, whom we met in Chapter 3, recalls an invitation-only roundtable gathering hosted by a private foundation in 2012. "The notion of it was 'Let's bring together all the big faith-at-work leaders and leaders of these marketplace ministries,'" says Sherman. "Of twenty-five people, I was the only woman of either one or two." She also notes that the speaker lineups of the major marketplace ministry conferences heavily skew male. Further, both Alsdorf and Sherman note that many FAW groups launched in a time when strong cultural forces kept women out of full-time professional work. The ministries "still haven't found ways to incorporate women," says Sherman. "The general problem is that the evangelical subculture is lagging behind."

Reaching the "Spiritual Sex"

Here's the rub: If churches are called to serve and bless their neighbors, to bear witness to the power of the gospel in all realms of life, then they will need to know how to serve and bless these women.

Granted, very few women in our neighborhoods will helm a corporation. Very few *people* will. In this regard, Katherine Leary Alsdorf has been a minority within a minority her entire professional life. But more women are launching small businesses and publishing research papers and writing for national publications and dreaming up nonprofits and generally shaping our communities and cultures in powerful ways. And they will, like Katherine, need a faith that makes sense of the very things they sense they were put on earth to do—even if they don't yet know who put them on earth to do them.

This is the very reason why Katherine decided to explore Christianity further. "I was a single woman whose life was 90 percent wrapped up in my work," she said. "If Christianity had not embraced the huge portion of our life which is work, I can't imagine that I would have responded in any way whatsoever."

Or, as Dorothy Sayers wrote, "How can anyone remain interested in a religion which seems to have no concern with nine-tenths of his [or her!] life?" She goes on:

> It is the business of the Church to recognize that the secular vocation, as such, is sacred: Christian people, and particularly perhaps the Christian clergy, must get it firmly into their heads that when a man or woman is called to a particular job of secular nature, that is as true a vocation as though he or she were called to specifically religious work.

Our ability to speak meaningfully into women's professional lives comes down to effective evangelism. If you want to know what the church could look like in a hundred years, find out where the women are. Women play such a crucial role in Christianity that some theologians have decried the "feminization" of the faith and a corresponding marginalization of men. Leon Podles, in the hallmark of the genre, *The Church Impotent: The Feminization of Christianity*, argues that churches started to become feminized in the thirteenth century, when some mystics and theologians began describing the soul's relationship to

God in romantic terms. Today, more women than men identify as evangelical Christians (55 versus 44 percent), and women of all stripes are considered the "spiritual sex." They are more likely to be certain there's a God, to pray daily, to say religious life is "very important," and to attend worship at least weekly. According to one Barna Group survey, in 80 percent of cases, women are the ones to decide whether a family will attend church. Which means they decide whether the youngest generation will be exposed to the faith.

Whether or not a church or denomination ordains women or permits them to preach, women have always crucially sustained the life of the local church. They have prayed and counseled and cooked meals and visited the sick and played the organ and taught the Bible and cared for children and managed the finances. Whether or not they lead the liturgy, they *do* the liturgy—the work of the people that sustains Christian life.

With growing educational attainment and professional success, more women will want to know that their work outside the church, and whatever gifts they exercise there, *matter* to their Christian brothers and sisters; that what they do at the office is no less formative or good than what they do inside the walls of the church. In fact, their work may be the place where their skills and training and passions are best used to bless their neighbors and witness to the God who calls work good.

I recognize that some of my readers will belong to church traditions that believe the roles of the pastor, minister, or authority figure in the local church fall to men. I believe that the vast majority of my fellow Christians who hold this conviction come to it in good conscience. They believe it because of a certain but credible and time-tested interpretation of Scripture, not due to sexism or a view of women as spiritually second-rate. I recognize that some of these readers might believe I am trying to get churches to empower women. They are right.

But not in a way that would undermine the convictions of mainstream complementarians. The call to vocationally equip and empower women for fruitfulness in the workplace transcends long-standing debates about women's proper function in the church. Why? Because we are not talking about the church gathered. We are talking about women in the world, the place where Christ calls all of us to go "and preach the gospel to all creation" (Mark 16:15; John 3:16). Even if women can't preach from the pulpit, all women are called to preach Christ—by sharing the gospel with colleagues, by treating coworkers with dignity and care, by contributing creatively to a community and professional field, by stewarding all of creation alongside men, reflecting the image of God in the way that Genesis describes the world as it was meant to be.

What All Churches Can Do

If you are reading this as a church leader and feeling overwhelmed by the task of equipping and empowering the Katherines in your midst, I have good news. Most women aren't looking to be praised in your next sermon. They don't want to act like men or forsake the calls to marriage and motherhood. They might actually love to bake cupcakes for the ministry fair—even while they manage a $500 million portfolio during the week.

The women I interviewed provided plenty of practical ways churches could equip and empower them to flourish at work. Here are some:

First, any time pastors or leaders talk about a congregant from the stage or pulpit, they get to shape church members' worldviews simply through *whom* they highlight and *what* they highlight. Thus, if a pastor wants to preach on the importance of women's professional work, he can speak volumes by highlighting a woman in the congregation.

Dorcas Cheng-Tozun, whom we heard from in Chapter 6, suggests that pastors include "examples of professional women and their struggles/victories in sermons and teachings." This helps to "normalize the professional roles that women have." By contrast, if a pastor or church leader highlights only male members in teachings on professional work, he subtly communicates that work is a thing for dudes.

Churches can also offer classes on work and vocation for all members. Sarah Pulliam Bailey, a religion reporter for *The Washington Post*, notes that an Indianapolis-based church she and her husband attended had a vocation Sunday school class that ended up being "really stimulating." "Too often we separate into gender-specific groups, which can be helpful for certain kinds of conversations," Bailey says. "But in this case, it was helpful to hear how both men and women faced similar challenges in their work."

Likewise, Jen Pollock Michel notes that Grace Toronto Church (PCA) hosts one or two annual work-related gatherings centered on professional fields rather than gender. "They always have something for people in business, law, and the arts," based on Redeemer Church's Center for Faith and Work model, she said. (She does lament that they have never hosted anything for caregivers—people who spend their time and energy ensuring that the vulnerable among us can flourish. Cue the church book club on Anne-Marie Slaughter's *Unfinished Business*.)

An easy fix for all churches: Host women's Bible studies at different times of the week.

Publicly naming members' skill sets and gifts can be another way churches communicate that they really see their members, whether or not those gifts are used in the church. Kate Shellnutt, a fellow editor at *Christianity Today*, observes that her former church "mentions a person's specific gifts . . . and their occupations when introducing new members before the church body." "I find this particularly affirming because it means the pastor actually knows what you do for a living," she says, "and now the rest of the congregation does, too." This allows the church to highlight all the professional fields its members inhabit Monday through Saturday.

Even at churches that believe that preaching the Word and administering Communion are roles reserved for men, there are plenty of ways to draw on the female members' vocational gifts. Many women I spoke with lamented that they were asked to serve in children's ministry or hospitality when they—and the church—would have been ten times better off with them giving advice on the payroll or the new building plan. As a counterexample, Ruth López Turley (whom we met at the end of Chapter 2) was *seen* for her actual gifts and training—sociological research on public education—and then asked to enrich the church's ministry based on those gifts. Imagine all the other ways the church would be enriched and blessed if it saw and then invited the gifts of women in the pews.

What We All Can Do

Even if church communities don't or can't find ways to vocationally equip women, we can equip one another. (Here's where I would like to insert a recording of myself singing "Circle of Friends," by Point of Grace.)

If you've reached the end of this book and are dying to discuss it: Go do it! Start talking to your friends, your spouse, your parents, your boss, your pastor—anyone who has an interest in seeing women blossom at work—about your response to A *Woman's Place*. Say what inspired you, frustrated you, piqued your curiosity, or simply made you want to keep thinking and praying about your own career. The most influential books do not become so because people read them but because people talk about them. I believe any shift around our conceptions of work and of women will come from these conversations, in which we find ways to equip women to pursue shalom on the job as in every other realm of life.

If you need help imagining some of these ways, here are specific recommendations:

Parents: Talk regularly with your children about the goodness of work: about our Worker God and his call to his image bearers to reign over his creation. In age-appropriate ways, help them understand what the gospel means both for their own souls and also for all people, places, and times.

For parents of a girl: Find ways to name her gifts, talents, and creativity, especially if those gifts and talents fall outside what's normal for or expected of girls. If your child excels at science and math, consider sending her to a summer camp; if she loves to shoot hoops (or play chess), help her find a team where she can be practice the dual gifts of competition and camaraderie. Talk regularly about how her gifts and talents might lead to a specific line of work or passion down the road. Simply ask her: "What do you want to be? To do?"

Most of all: Enjoy *your* work, and talk about why you do. Model having a calling and vocation that's distinct from your children but contributes to their well-being. Many, many women I spoke with this for this book said they are better mothers when they are investing in a passion or pursuit outside their family. Embody multiple callings.

Educators: If you work on a college campus, you have a front-row seat for the vocational blossoming of the women and men who will go on to lead our institutions and shape our culture in profound ways. Yet for many female students I spoke with, there remains a gap between colleges' mission statements and their practice in young women's lives. If you work for a college, consider creating special programs that ensure young women can be world changers—in their own corner of the world, of course—after graduation. That could be discernment groups for women in the dorms or in off-campus coffee shops; panel discussions featuring faculty on how they have navigated work and family simultaneously; group "ask us anything" discussions with married faculty couples on how they have pursued two careers at once; mentor-matching programs with female faculty; courses or informal discussions on workplace leadership, ambition, and dealing with discrimination and gender barriers on the job.

On a more informal level, male faculty and staff might discern ways to invest as much in their female students as in their male students, ensuring that they aren't overlooking female students to avoid the appearance of indiscretion. If you're a male teacher and you need an open-door policy, consider applying it to your male students, too. If you need to refer your female students to female faculty in your department, try to do so in a way that doesn't subtly shame your students.

In all activities, don't waste the precious opportunity of higher education to set women on paths of professional fruitfulness.

Bosses: If you have any influence over your company's or organization's policies, ask some questions about your workplace: Does our employee manual explicitly commit itself to creating a pro-woman, pro-family culture? Does the manual include up-to-date policies on flexible work hours, paid maternity leave, paid paternity leave, and/or proactively promoting women to leadership roles? How many women in the organization's leadership can you name? If you struggle to think of more than a few, ask yourself why that is. Consider going to your supervisor, other top leadership, or the board to request that gender equity be made a core commitment. Especially if you work for a faith-based organization, consider the scriptural resources that dictate employees be rewarded according to each person's variety of gifts and contributions to the common good, not according to a "flesh-based" preference for men over women.

If you have female employees, ask: What kind of opportunities for advancement or growth is she receiving? Are they commensurate with her title and position? With her potential and personal goals? With those of male employees at the same level?

Do men speak over her or interrupt her in meetings and decision-making conversations? Is she officially included but unofficially left out of hallway conversation or office banter? Is coarse and sexual humor tolerated? If so, is that negatively affecting her on-the-job performance and demeanor? What can you do to stop or counteract sexist behavior, whether it's overt or quiet?

You: After having just read a book about work, the last thing you need to do is sit someplace and think about work. However, I have found that women (especially those with young children) can face guilt for thinking too much or too seriously about their own career aspirations and callings. To counteract misplaced guilt, consider taking a "vocation retreat"—by yourself, unplugged, away from friends and family and the din of social media. Set aside that time to be with God, to lay before him your latent vocational hopes and life course. Write down the times in your life when, to paraphrase Frederick Buechner, your heart's deep gladness and the world's deep needs meet in space and time. What *are* your heart's deep gladnesses? What are your world's deep needs? Ask God to reveal how they might intersect in ways you might not have considered or imagined.

Keep naming—to your husband, friends, counselor, pastor, or life coach—what it is you actually *want* to do on the next leg of your vocational journey. Even if those longings are not realizable now or for a long time, there is power in naming them. In having others see and call out your gifts and offerings and how they might bless others. In getting honest with yourself that you *have* the desire to put your hand to the plow, to play your part in the spread of shalom, to use your ambitions for God and his kingdom.

After his major theological shift around the eternal value of our work, Tom Nelson (the Kansas City pastor whom we heard from earlier) noticed that Christ Community Church's "cultural icons and cultural language" began to shift. They began commissioning different individuals and different vocations, and they began using prayers to honor and bless labor. One of their regular benedictions— the prayer of blessing over worshippers at the end of a service—is Psalm 90:17:

May the favor of the Lord our God rest on us;
Establish the work of our hands for us—
Yes, establish the work of our hands.

God made us rulers over the works of his hands. As we go about our work, he is mindful of us; he cares for us (Ps. 8). When we recover this vision for all Christians, I imagine that more and more women will find God's favor resting upon them.

K.B.

ACKNOWLEDGMENTS

This book wouldn't exist without Chris Park, an agent who is fierce and gentle in equal and perfect proportion; Becky Nesbitt, the Howard editor who saw promise in my idea, and Beth Adams, the Howard editor who saw the idea to completion; the many women who hosted or coordinated group conversations—Jennifer Trafton Peterson, Tamara Hill Murphy, Andrea Palpant Dilley, Christy Tennant Krispin, Ruth Moon, Laura Ortberg Turner, Sarah Pulliam Bailey, Megan Slaboda, Stacy Bartholemew, Rachel Marie Stone, and Morna Comeau; the many women who participated in the conversations—this book wouldn't exist without your time, stories, and vulnerability; Hannah Anderson, Helen Lee, and Karen Swallow Prior, who provided invaluable feedback on an early draft; the Her.manas, and your beautifully written prayers, plus all the giggles; Sarah, Chris, and the babes—love you so much; Mom, Dad, Nonnie, and Mookie, for your constant care, support, and prayers; and to the One who has sustained me through the writing project, even more than La Croix sparkling water. You are faithful, and this book is for your honor and glory. Thank you.

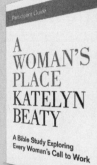

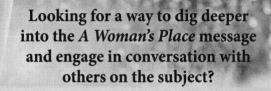